SOUL
KEEPING

STUDY GUIDE

Resources by John Ortberg

Everybody's Normal Till You Get to Know Them
(book, ebook, audio)

God Is Closer Than You Think
(book, ebook, audio, curriculum with Stephen and Amanda Sorenson)

*If You Want to Walk on Water,
You've Got to Get Out of the Boat*
(book, ebook, audio, curriculum with Stephen and Amanda Sorenson)

Know Doubt
(book, ebook, previously titled *Faith and Doubt*)

The Life You've Always Wanted
(book, ebook, audio, curriculum with Stephen and Amanda Sorenson)

Love Beyond Reason

The Me I Want to Be
(book, ebook, audio, curriculum with Scott Rubin)

Soul Keeping
(book, ebook, curriculum with Christine M. Anderson)

When the Game Is Over, It All Goes Back in the Box
(book, ebook, audio, curriculum with Stephen and Amanda Sorenson)

Who Is This Man?
(book, ebook, audio, curriculum with Christine M. Anderson)

SOUL KEEPING

CARING *for* THE MOST IMPORTANT PART *of* YOU

JOHN ORTBERG

WITH CHRISTINE M. ANDERSON

ZONDERVAN®

ZONDERVAN

Soul Keeping Study Guide
Copyright © 2014 by John Ortberg

This title is also available as a Zondervan ebook. Visit www.zondervan.com/ebooks.

Requests for information should be addressed to:

Zondervan, 3900 *Sparks Dr. SE, Grand Rapids, MI 49546*

ISBN 978-0-310-69127-3

Cover design: Curt Diepenhorst
Cover photography: Tolga Sipahi / Getty Images®
Interior design: Beth Shagene

Printed in the United States of America

14 15 16 17 18 19 20 /DCI/ 22 21 20 19 18 17 16 15 14 13 12 11 10 9 8 7 6 5 4

CONTENTS

HOW TO USE
THIS GUIDE

Group Size

The *Soul Keeping* video study is designed to be experienced in a group setting such as a Bible study, Sunday school class, or any small group gathering. To ensure everyone has enough time to participate in discussions, it is recommended that large groups break up into smaller groups of four to six people each.

Materials Needed

Each participant should have his or her own study guide, which includes notes for video segments, directions for activities and discussion questions, as well as personal studies to deepen learning between sessions.

Timing

The time notations—for example (25 minutes)—indicate the *actual* time of video segments and the *suggested* times for each activity or discussion. For example:

Individual Activity: **What I Want to Remember** (2 minutes)

Adhering to the suggested times will enable you to complete each session in ninety minutes. If you have just one hour for your meeting, you will need to choose fewer questions for discussion. You may also opt to devote two meetings rather than one to each session. In addition to allowing discussions to be more spacious, this has the added advantage of allowing group members to read related chapters in the *Soul Keeping* book and to complete the personal study between meetings. In the second meeting, devote the time allotted for watching the video to discussing group members' insights and questions from their reading and personal study.

Group Practice

Each session ends with a suggested application activity for group members to complete between sessions. Although the activity is completed outside of the group meeting, it's a good idea to read through the group practice before concluding the meeting to clarify any questions and to make sure everyone is on board.

Facilitation

Each group should appoint a facilitator who is responsible for starting the video and for keeping track of time during discussions and activities. Facilitators may also read questions aloud and monitor discussions, prompting participants to respond and ensuring that everyone has the opportunity to participate.

Personal Studies

Maximize the impact of the curriculum with additional study between group sessions. Every personal study includes reflection questions as well as a Bible study and a guided prayer activity based on a psalm. You'll get the most out of the study by setting aside about thirty minutes between sessions for personal study, as well as additional time to complete the group practice activity.

WHAT IS THE SOUL?

Our soul is like an inner stream of water, which gives strength, direction, and harmony to every other element of our life. When that stream is as it should be, we are constantly refreshed and exuberant in all we do, because our soul itself is then profusely rooted in the vastness of God and his kingdom, including nature; and all else within us is enlivened and directed by that stream. Therefore we are in harmony with God, reality, and the rest of human nature and nature at large.

DALLAS WILLARD, *RENOVATION OF THE HEART*

Welcome!

Welcome to Session 1 of *Soul Keeping*. Each of the six sessions in this study is designed to be completed in ninety minutes. If you have just one hour for your meeting, you will need to choose fewer questions for your discussion. You may also opt to devote two meetings rather than one to each session.

If this is your first time together as a group, take a moment to introduce yourselves to each other before watching the video. Then let's begin!

Video: What Is the Soul? (25 minutes)

Play the video segment for Session 1. As you watch, use the outline provided to follow along or to take additional notes on anything that stands out to you.

Notes

The Parable of the Keeper of the Stream

Questions about the human soul:

What is it?

What does it consist of?

Why does it matter, if it *does* matter?

Is it doing okay?

All of us have an outer life and an inner life.

My outer life is the public, visible me — my accomplishments, my work, my reputation.

My inner life is largely invisible. It's where my secret thoughts, hopes, and wishes live.

"What matters most, what marks your existence, the really deep reason why human life matters so much, is because of this tiny, fragile, vulnerable, precious thing about you called your soul. You are not just a self; you are a soul. You are a soul made by God, made for God, and made to need God, made to run on God. Which means that you are not made to be self-sufficient" (Dallas Willard).

The self is not the soul.

In the twentieth century, we replaced community, society, church, and faith with a tiny little unit that cannot bear the weight of meaning. We've replaced all these larger entities with the *self*.

The self is a stand-alone, do-it-yourself unit, while the soul reminds us we are not made for ourselves or by ourselves. The soul always exists before God.

Your soul connects your thoughts, your sensations, your emotions, your will, and integrates them into an entire being.

The four parts of a human being

Each part of a human being must be healthy and working as God intended it to, and that makes a healthy soul.

Will: The innermost circle is the will—the capacity to choose. The will is what makes you a person and not a thing. It is important but it is also extremely limited.

Mind: The second circle is the mind, a person's thoughts and feelings.

"The mind of the sinful [person] is death, but the mind controlled by the Spirit is life and peace" (Romans 8:6 NIV 1984).

Body: The third circle is the body.

"Our bodies are like our little power packs—we couldn't be us without them.... But they are not the whole story. We are not just the stuff that our bodies are made of" (Dallas Willard).

(Soul:)The final circle is the soul. The human soul is what integrates all of our different parts into a single person. *why human life matters: you are a soul made by God, made for God, made to need God, made to run on God our soul gives strength, direction and harmony to every other element of our life - a healthy center that organizes and directs my life p. 32 -*

"A healthy soul is an integrated soul, and an unhealthy soul is a 'dis-integrated' one" (Dallas Willard).

When we're dealing with a disintegrated soul, we have to come to grips with sin.

What does it mean to lose one's soul?

"What good will it be for someone to gain the whole world, yet forfeit their soul?" (Matthew 16:26).

What Jesus is saying is a diagnostic expression. To lose my soul means I no longer have a healthy center that organizes and guides my life.

You have a soul, and for you to have a soul that is healed, that is healthy, that is redeemed by God, matters more than the outcome of any circumstance in your world or your life. Your eternal destiny rests on the well-being of your soul—and only God can heal the soul.

What does it mean to "keep" one's soul?

"You must ruthlessly eliminate hurry from your life.... Hurry is the great enemy of souls in our day. Being busy is mostly a condition of our outer world; it's having many things to do. Being hurried is a problem of the soul. It's being so preoccupied with myself and what myself has to do that I am no longer able to be fully present with God and others. There is no way a soul can thrive when it is hurried. And nobody will come along and unhurry your soul for you" (Dallas Willard).

You have one soul; and gaining the whole world will not help you if you lose it.

Caring for your soul, allowing it to flourish in God's presence and become a gift to the world around you, is the primary charge that faces you before eternity.

"This is the most important thing you can know about your identity: You are an unceasing spiritual being with an eternal destiny in God's great universe" (Dallas Willard).

Your soul will live forever — and you are the keeper of your soul.

Group Discussion (63 minutes)

Take time to talk about what you just watched.

1. What part of the teaching had the most impact on you?

You Are the Keeper

2. A keeper is someone who is in charge of caring for, maintaining, or protecting something. For example, there are innkeepers, zookeepers, bookkeepers, groundskeepers, housekeepers, peacekeepers, shopkeepers, gatekeepers, beekeepers, etc.

 • Along with the parable John told about the keeper of the stream, what do these images of keepers suggest about the tasks and characteristics of "keeping" in general? For example, the stream keeper's work was described as "unseen."

 • What comes to mind when you think of these characteristics in connection with your soul? In other words, what might they reveal about what it means for you to engage in soul keeping?

How: Caring

maintaining

protecting

Describing the Soul

3. It can be hard to define the soul, but sometimes we have moments when we recognize it even if we can't define it. For example, John described feeling "an enormous combination of joy and humility and awe" when he watches a sunset at Big Sur, and how there is a depth to that experience that goes beyond what he can apprehend visually.

 • Think back over the last day or two. In what moments did you catch a glimpse of your soul at work? (If nothing comes to mind, think back to the most recent experience you can recall.)

- How, specifically, do you recognize your soul in these moments? In other words, what distinguishes these moments from other moments?

- Overall, would you say you tend to be more aware of your soul in uplifting experiences (such as the one John described) or in experiences of hardship and suffering? Share the reasons for your response.

4. The Bible doesn't provide a comprehensive definition of the soul, but the words biblical writers use offer insights about its meaning. In the Old Testament, the Hebrew word for the soul is *nephesh* (neh'-fesh). New Testament writers use the Greek word *psyche* (psü-khā') to name the soul. The root words for both *nephesh* and *psyche* refer to "breath."

Nephesh can be translated in several ways, but it is commonly rendered *life* or *soul*. For example:

> The ransom for a life [*nephesh*] is costly, no payment is ever enough. (Psalm 49:8)

> Only take care, and keep your soul [*nephesh*] diligently. (Deuteronomy 4:9a ESV)

Psyche is also frequently translated as *life* or *soul*. We see both uses in this statement made by Jesus:

> For whoever wants to save their life [*psyche*] will lose it, but whoever loses their life [*psyche*] for me will find it. What good will it be for someone to gain the whole world, yet forfeit their soul [*psyche*]? Or what can anyone give in exchange for their soul [*psyche*]? (Matthew 16:25–26)

In biblical usage, *nephesh* and *psyche* are words that encompass

nephesh + psyche

all that makes a person a living being, "summing up ... the whole personality, of the whole self of a person."[1] In essence, they are words that refer to your life as an integrated whole and all the components that make you uniquely *you*.

- Briefly reflect on the soul using the image of breath, the meaning of the biblical root words. For example, you might consider when you tend to be most and least aware of your physical breathing, what takes your breath away, or what makes you hold your breath. What parallels do you recognize between these physical experiences of breath and the ways in which you might experience, or fail to experience, your soul at work?

- The three Scriptures quoted above stress the incalculable value of the soul and the importance of making an intentional effort to care for it. And yet, as Dallas Willard acknowledged, even among Christians, "very few people [are] seriously concerned about the state of their own soul."[2] Overall, how would you assess yourself in this regard? For example, would you say the attention and care you give to the state of your soul right now is the highest it's ever been, the lowest, or somewhere between? Share the reasons for your response.

Caring for the Soul

5. John described a distinction Dallas Willard made between being busy and being hurried:

Hurry is the great enemy of souls in our day. Being busy is mostly

1. Colin Brown, "Soul," *New International Dictionary of New Testament Theology*, vol. 3, Colin Brown, gen. ed. (Grand Rapids: Zondervan, 1978, 1986), 680.
2. Dallas Willard, *Renovation of the Heart*, 208.

a condition of our outer world; it is having many things to do. Being hurried is a problem of the soul. It's being so preoccupied with myself and what myself has to do that I am no longer able to be fully present with God and fully present with you. There is no way a soul can thrive when it is hurried.

- How would you assess the threat level of hurry to your soul right now? Is it very high, moderate, or low?

- When are you most likely to succumb to hurry—to lose the ability to be fully present with God and others?

- If you were to describe the characteristics of a person who is busy but *not* hurried, what would they be? For example, what would you expect to notice about their demeanor, their actions, and their interactions with others?

6. John said that this was the most important thing he had to say:

> You have a soul, and for you to have a soul that is healed, that is healthy, that is redeemed by God, matters more than the outcome of any circumstance in your world or your life. Your eternal destiny rests on the well-being of your soul—and only God can heal the soul.

In what ways might the next twenty-four hours be different if you were to take this statement seriously? For example, how might it influence the decisions you make, the way you spend your time, or the way you relate to others?

Souls in Community

7. In addition to learning about *Soul Keeping* together as a group, it's important to also be aware of how God is at work among you—especially in how you relate to each other and share your lives throughout the study. As you discuss the teaching in each session, there will be many opportunities to speak life-giving—and life-challenging—words, and to listen to one another deeply. Being with each other in this way doesn't happen by accident. Dallas Willard writes:

> Persons rarely become present where they are not heartily wanted. Certainly that is true for you and me. We prefer to be wanted, warmly wanted, before we reveal our souls—or even come to a party.[3]

As you anticipate the next several weeks of learning together in community, what would help you to "become present" within the group? Use one or more of the sentence starters below, or your own statement, to help the group understand the best way to be a good companion to you throughout this study. As each person responds, use the two-page chart that follows to briefly note what is important to that person and how you can be a good companion to them.

I feel "heartily wanted" in a group when ...

It really helps me to become present when ...

I tend to withdraw or feel anxious when ...

I'd like you to consistently challenge me about ...

You can help me to take my soul seriously by ...

In our discussions, the best thing you could do for me is ...

---

3. Dallas Willard, *The Divine Conspiracy* (San Francisco: HarperSanFrancisco, 1998), 77.

Name	The Best Way I Can Be a Good Companion to This Person ...

Name	The Best Way I Can Be a Good Companion to This Person ...

Individual Activity: What I Want to Remember (2 minutes)

Complete this activity on your own.

1. Briefly review the video outline and any notes you took.

2. In the space below, write down the most significant thing you gained in this session—from the teaching, activities, or discussions.

What I want to remember from this session . . .

Group Practice: Attending to the Soul

Each session in the *Soul Keeping* study includes a group practice that each of you will complete on your own between sessions, then debrief together at the start of the next meeting. Although the practice is completed outside of the group gathering, it's a good idea to read through the practice description before concluding your meeting each week. In some cases, activities will require preparation or setting aside time each day to complete. As part of attending to the soul, it's important not to hurry or try to complete activities at the last minute.

The group practice for this week is to spend time each day attending to your soul. When we attend to something, we think about it, listen to it, watch it carefully. We are generous with full and thoughtful attention. The purpose of this practice is not to "do" or achieve anything but simply to become increasingly aware of your soul in the course of everyday life. Here are two options for ways to attend to your soul between now and your next group meeting.

- **Option 1:** Set aside fifteen minutes at the beginning or end of each day to reflect on the previous twenty-four hours. In what two or three moments do you recognize your soul at work? For example, it might be an experience of beauty or connection to God; an experience of suffering; or a time when you felt an internal conflict (between your will, your mind, and/or your body). How specifically do you recognize your soul — rather than your "self" — in this experience? Briefly note your responses on a pad of paper or in a journal. At the end of the week, review your daily responses. What stands out most to you about the times you recognize your soul at work?

- **Option 2:** Each day, set a timer or an alert (on your watch, smartphone, laptop, etc.) for two or three intervals throughout the day. For example at 10:00 a.m., 3:00 p.m., 7:00 p.m., or perhaps around meal times. At each interval, allow five minutes to turn your attention to your soul. Ask, *What does my soul need right now? How is it different from what my "self" thinks it needs right now?* Note your responses with a brief line or two on a pad of paper or in a journal (or email them to yourself). At the end of the week, review your daily notes. What stands out most to you about what your soul routinely needs or about the differences between the needs of your soul and the needs of your self?

With either option, you may find it helpful to first review the Session 1 personal study, which includes additional information about the four dimensions of the person — the will, the mind, the body, and the soul.

Bring your notes from the week to the next group gathering. You'll have a chance to talk about your experiences and observations at the beginning of the Session 2 discussion.

Closing Prayer

Close your time together with prayer.

SESSION 1: Personal Study

Read and Learn

Read the prologue, introduction, and chapters 1–2 of the book *Soul Keeping*. Use the space below to note any insights or questions you want to bring to the next group session.

Study and Reflect

> Your soul is what integrates your will (your intentions), your mind (your thoughts and feelings, your values and conscience), and your body (your face, body language, and actions) into a single life. A soul is healthy — well-ordered — when there is harmony between these three entities and God's intent for all creation. When you are connected with God and other people in life, you have a healthy soul.
>
> *Soul Keeping*, page 39

1. It is very important to understand the "parts" of the inner life. In order to care for the soul, we have to understand what it is made of and how it works. The pages that follow provide an overview of the four parts or dimensions of the human being: the *will*, the *mind*, the *body*, and the *soul*. For each dimension, there is a brief definition and a chart that describes what that dimension looks like when it is disintegrated (unhealthy) and integrated (healthy).[4] Read through the definition and the chart for each dimension, underlining any words or phrases that stand out to you. Then use the chart as a reference in responding to the corresponding sentence starters.

---

4. Definitions and content in the four charts is adapted from *Renovation of the Heart* by Dallas Willard and *Soul Keeping* by John Ortberg.

The Will

The function of the will is to organize our life as a whole, and to organize it around God. The will includes our intentions, choices, decisions, and character. It is our will that has the power to do what is good or evil. We exercise the will primarily in the power to select what we think on and how intently we will focus on it — from which our other decisions and actions then more or less directly flow.

I recognize the *disintegration* of my will in these ways (specific habits, thoughts/feelings, reactions, experiences, choices, relationships, etc.) ...

I recognize the *integration* of my will in these ways ...

Characteristics of the Disintegrated Will	Characteristics of the Integrated Will
• The constant character of the will apart from God is chaotic duplicity and confusion. It wills many things and they cannot be reconciled with each other. • We are enslaved to our own self-conflicted will. • Our will is organized around feelings or desires rather than God. • Our will is shrouded in layer upon layer of destructive habits. • Our drive toward good is splintered, corrupted, and eventually turned against ourselves. • The key question is: "How can I get my way?" • We routinely engage in manipulation, deception, seduction, malice, and exaltation of self. • Deception—pretending to feel and think one way while acting another—is often self-deception.	• The character of the healthy will is a single-minded and joyous devotion to God and his will, to what God wants for us—and to service to him and to others because of him. • The will is not at war with itself and is capable of directing all of the parts of the self in harmony with one another under the direction of God. • The key question is: "What good can I bring about?" • We reach out to God in trust. • We place our confidence entirely in God and surrender to God's supremacy in all things. • Our lives and interactions are routinely characterized by transparency, sincerity, goodwill, submission, and service to God. • We are abandoned to God and content with the will of God. • We do not hesitate to do what is right.

The Mind

The mind includes our thoughts, memories, ideas, feelings, values, desires, conscience, reasoning, perceptions, beliefs, and imagination, etc. The power we have over our thoughts assists us in directing and controlling our feelings, which are not directly under the guidance of our will.

I recognize the *disintegration* of my mind in these ways (specific habits, thoughts/feelings, reactions, experiences, choices, relationships, etc.) ...

I recognize the *integration* of my mind in these ways ...

Characteristics of the Disintegrated Mind	Characteristics of the Integrated Mind
• The mind apart from God becomes a wild mix of thought and feeling manifested in willful stupidities, blatant inconsistencies, and confusions.	• The healthy mind is being constantly transformed and renewed (Romans 12:2). It is increasingly characterized by hope, faith, love, joy, and peace.
• We equate God with our limited ideas about God, and so fail to know what God is really like and what his law requires (Hosea 4:6).	• We desire to be conformed to the mind of Christ, and move toward a total exchange of our own ideas and images for his.
• We actively crowd God out of our thoughts, and the mind is trapped by destructive ideas and images about both God and ourselves.	• We apply our mind to truth by consistently taking in the Word of God, dwelling on it, pondering its meaning, and exploring its implications for our lives.
• We are mastered and enslaved by feelings and believe our feelings must be satisfied. The mind is set on the flesh, which is death (Romans 8:6).	• We fill our mind with thoughts of truth and beauty, desiring what is wholesome and good.
• We cannot distinguish between our feelings and our will.	• We know and accept the fact that our feelings do not have to be satisfied.
• We lack self-control, which turns life into a mere drift.	• We have a compelling vision of ourselves as becoming free from our besetting sins. We are open to radical change in ourselves, to careful and creative instruction, and to divine grace.
• We cannot envision who we would be without the fears, angers, lusts, power ploys, and woundedness with which we have lived so long. We identify with our habit-worn feelings.	• We exhibit self-control and can accomplish what we have decided to do and be, even when we "don't feel like it."
• We are obsessed with and blinded by negative thoughts and feelings.	• We have learned to reason with, be critical of, and have some distance from our thoughts and feelings.

The Body

The body is our primary energy source and the focal point of our presence in the physical and social world. It includes our facial expressions, body language, actions, and interactions with the world around us. The body is the original and primary place of our dominion and our responsibility. In union with it, we come into existence and become the person we will forever be.

I recognize the *disintegration* of my body in these ways (specific habits, thoughts/feelings, reactions, experiences, choices, relationships, etc.) ...

I recognize the *integration* of my body in these ways ...

Characteristics of the Disintegrated Body	Characteristics of the Integrated Body
• The body becomes a primary barrier to conformity to Christ and hinders us from doing what we know to be good and right.	• The body becomes our primary ally in Christlikeness and a showplace of God's greatness (1 Corinthians 6:19–20).
• The role of the body is distorted as it becomes a primary source of gratification and instrument for getting what we want. This results in "death" and alienation from God (Galatians 6:8).	• We release the body to God's care and no longer idolize, worship, or misuse it.
• Taking the body as a main concern makes it impossible to please God and at the same time ensures the utter futility of our life (Romans 8:5–7).	• The body is properly honored, cared for, and regarded as holy because it is inhabited by God (Romans 8:11).
• We become a slave to our appetites (Romans 16:18). The body is idolized, worshiped, and misused.	• The body is increasingly able to do the things that Jesus did and taught (Romans 8:4).
• The body is a source of fear, shame, disgust, agitation, anger, and self-loathing.	• The body becomes the easy servant of the integrated mind and will.
• Bodily pleasure is exalted to a necessity and we become dependent on it.	• The body is filled with appetites that serve the good and with habits that lead to excellent living.
• The body acts wrongly "before we think," and in opposition to the Spirit (Galatians 5:17).	• The body becomes a "[slave] to righteousness leading to holiness" (Romans 6:19).
• Parts of the body feel beyond our control and engage in sins of their own: a lying tongue, haughty eyes, hands that shed innocent blood, feet that rush to do evil (Proverbs 6:17–18).	• We take responsibility to care for our body, but view the body as God's to do with as he pleases (1 Corinthians 6:19–20).

The Soul

The soul is that dimension of the person that interrelates all of the other dimensions so that they form one life. The soul is the most basic level of life in the individual, and one that is by nature rooted in God. It is also the deepest part of the person and has the capacity to operate without conscious supervision.

I recognize the *disintegration* of my soul in these ways (specific habits, thoughts/feelings, reactions, experiences, choices, relationships, etc.) ...

I recognize the *integration* of my soul in these ways ...

Characteristics of the Disintegrated Soul	Characteristics of the Integrated Soul
• The soul apart from God mistakes itself for God. As a result, everything becomes delusional. • We are dead in trespasses and sins, enslaved to desires or bodily habits, or blinded by false ideas, distorted images, and misinformation. • We are displaced and disoriented. We do not know where we are or how to get where we want to go. • We are locked in a self-destructive struggle with ourselves and with all those around us. • Our habitual condition is one of conflict and of acting other than how we ourselves intend or regard as wise. • Our inner condition makes it impossible for us to deal with the demands of life. We cannot "get it all together." • Performance is at a premium because life lacks meaning. • Sin and disobedience make it impossible for our soul to rest. Sinful desires war against the soul (1 Peter 2:11). • We struggle with life on our own.	• The healthy soul is one in which all the essential parts of the human being are organized around God, as they are restored and sustained by him. This is what it means to be fully integrated under God. • We embrace an overall, settled condition of life in the kingdom of God described as death to self (Matthew 16:24–25). • We are prepared for and capable of responding to the situations of life in ways that are good and right. • Whatever the circumstances, we are enabled by Christ to rest in the Lord and wait patiently for him (Psalm 37:7). We abandon outcomes to God. • We do not have to look out for ourselves because God is in charge of our life. • We live in pursuit of knowing Jesus Christ and are caught up in what he is doing (2 Corinthians 5:17; Philippians 3:10). • We seek to do everything in Jesus' name, knowing that what we do counts for eternity and is preserved there (Colossians 3:17).

2. Based on your responses to question 1, which number on the continuums below would you say best describes the degree to which you are experiencing integration or disintegration in the four dimensions of your life? Circle your response.

My Will

1	2	3	4	5	6	7	8	9	10

My will is
disintegrated
(unhealthy).

My will is
integrated
(healthy).

My Mind

1	2	3	4	5	6	7	8	9	10

My mind is
disintegrated
(unhealthy).

My mind is
integrated
(healthy).

My Body

1	2	3	4	5	6	7	8	9	10

My body is
disintegrated
(unhealthy).

My body is
integrated
(healthy).

My Soul

1	2	3	4	5	6	7	8	9	10

My soul is
disintegrated
(unhealthy).

My soul is
integrated
(healthy).

> The very first thing that we must do is to be mindful of our soul, to acknowledge it.... Once we clearly acknowledge the soul, we can learn to hear its cries.
>
> Dallas Willard, *Renovation of the Heart*, pages 207, 209

3. For many reasons, most of us find it difficult to truly attend to the soul—to acknowledge it and to give it the care it requires. The soul is quiet but also resilient, and it longs to be heard.

> *I have been waiting.*
>
> *I am shy—terribly shy—even in the most boisterous person. I can only whisper, never shout. You may never even notice me.*
>
> *But I am here, waiting.*
>
> *I do not lie on the surface. If you look and listen, patiently, you will know.*
>
> *I speak through your confusion, through your wanting, through your hurt. When you stammer, when you say what you did not mean to say, it was I. When you watch a sunset, or hear a child laugh, or listen to a piece of music that causes you to suddenly become choked up, it is I that causes your eyes to fill. When you are addicted, it is I that is chained.*
>
> *When the sun burns up and the universe melts away, I will be here. Like Glenn Close in the movie* Fatal Attraction, *I will not be ignored. I can be wounded, lost, repulsed, or redeemed. Your circumstances actually matter far less to your happiness than you think. It is my health that makes your life heaven or hell.*
>
> *I am your soul. I am here.*[5]

If this were your soul speaking to you, how would you respond? What would you want your soul to know?

---

5. *Soul Keeping,* pages 56–57.

4. Dallas Willard writes that "the indispensable first step in caring for the soul is to place it under God."[6] Read Psalm 24, which describes a soul completely at rest in God's care. Drawing on the psalm as a reference, use the space below to write your own prayer. Acknowledge the areas of your life where you are struggling with disintegration. Ask God to help you begin to recognize and attend to your soul. Place your soul under God by naming the ways in which you are surrendering yourself to his care.

---

6. Dallas Willard, *Renovation of the Heart*, 208.

THE STRUGGLE OF THE SOUL

The ruined life is not to be enhanced but replaced.
We must simply lose our life — that ruined life
about which most people complain so much anyway.
DALLAS WILLARD, *RENOVATION OF THE HEART*

Group Discussion: Checking In (20 minutes)

A key part of getting to know God better is sharing your journey with others. Before watching the video, check in with each other about your experiences since the last session. For example:

- Briefly share your experience of the Session 1 group practice. What did you learn or experience in your daily times of attending to your soul?

- What insights did you discover in the personal study or in the chapters you read from the book *Soul Keeping*?

- How did the last session impact your daily life or your relationship with God?

- What questions would you like to ask the other members of your group?

Video: The Struggle of the Soul (24 minutes)

Play the video segment for Session 2. As you watch, use the outline provided to follow along or to take additional notes on anything that stands out to you.

Notes

"Whoever wants to be my disciple must deny themselves and take up their cross daily and follow me" (Luke 9:23).

The Parable of the Soils (Matthew 13:3–9)

    The seed is a little picture of God's desire and action to redeem souls — to turn us from people who have trouble dying to self into people who live by dying to self.

The sower is God. The soil is a metaphor for the soul.

Hardened soil represents a soul that is cynical, bitter, or suspicious.

Rocky soil represents a soul that is shallow and settles for going through the motions.

Thorny soil represents a soul that chokes on the desire for things besides God.

Good soil represents a healthy soul.

We get to choose the kind of soul we have.

Jesus wants us to live with a healthy soul but much of the time we settle for living with a lost soul.

Sin splits the self.

"You desire truth in the inward parts," the psalmist said to God (Psalm 51:6 NKJV). That's soul talk—seed falling on good soil.

✳Even a single act of dishonesty shapes how we view ourselves. We are souls and everything is connected.

The soul is only able to bear so much truth. If I knew what it really would take to die to myself with any regularity, would I still want to follow Christ?

Francis Fénelon said, "God is merciful, showing us our true hideousness only in proportion to the courage he gives us to bear the sight."

"I remember my affliction ... the bitterness and the gall. I well remember them, and my soul is downcast within me" (Lamentations 3:19–20).

Our souls always crave the good soil.

The most important thing about you is not the thing that you achieve. It is the person that you become.

Group Discussion   (44 minutes)

Take time to talk about what you just watched.

1. What part of the teaching had the most impact on you?

The Difficulty of Dying to Self

2. At the beginning of the video, John described several of the ways he has failed to follow Jesus' command to deny oneself (Luke 9:23): jealousy of a ministry colleague, pleasure at telling a story that put someone else in a bad light, withdrawing from his wife when she challenged him.

Sometimes we face circumstances in which the choice to deny ourselves is fairly obvious. For example, we must choose whether or not to share financial resources, to honor one of the Ten Commandments, or to engage in self-destructive behavior. However, some of John's examples involved more subtle actions and choices, ones that offered what he called "plausible deniability."

- How would you describe the unique challenges posed by both obvious and subtle choices when it comes to denying oneself? As part of your discussion, consider this quote from author C. S. Lewis: "It is in some ways more troublesome to track and swat an evasive wasp than to shoot, at close range, a wild elephant. But the elephant is more troublesome if you miss."[7]

• Which would you say you tend to struggle with most right now—the subtle, "plausible deniability" choices, or the more obvious choices? What makes these choices especially difficult?

3. Choice is an essential component in following Jesus' command to die to self. Jesus taught and modeled this when he described his impending death to his disciples:

> I am the good shepherd. The good shepherd sacrifices his life for the sheep. . . . The Father loves me because I sacrifice my life so I may take it back again. No one can take my life from me. I sacrifice it voluntarily. For I have the authority to lay it down when I want to and also to take it up again. For this is what my Father has commanded. (John 10:11, 17–18 NLT)

Jesus' expectation for his followers is not that they will occasionally make a sacrificial choice, but that sacrificial choices will become a lifestyle:

> If any of you wants to be my follower, you must turn from your selfish ways, take up your cross daily, and follow me. If you try to hang on to your life, you will lose it. But if you give up your life for my sake, you will save it. (Luke 9:23–24 NLT)

---

7. C. S. Lewis, *The Screwtape Letters* (San Francisco: HarperSanFrancisco, 1942, 1996, 2001), 202.

By Jesus' definition, a cross is only a cross when we choose it—we could choose otherwise, but we make it a habit not to. For love of Christ, we consent to die to our self-serving ways—daily.

- A daily choice is a habit practiced in the routines of everyday life and relationships. As you think back over the last day or two, what opportunities did you have to take up your cross—to make a loving, sacrificial choice? Briefly identify one or two.

- At the time, did you recognize your response as a choice, or did it seem automatic, almost as if you didn't have a choice?

- In the Luke 9 passage, the phrase "for my sake" marks a significant qualification. How would you describe the differences between a sacrificial choice made for the sake of Christ and a sacrificial choice made for the sake of someone or something besides Christ?

- Do you think it's possible to make a sacrificial choice that is nevertheless selfish or self-serving? Share any examples you can think of to illustrate your response.

4. Part of the difficulty of dying to self is the fear that we are denying something essential about who we are or what's important to us. But Dallas Willard makes this important distinction:

> The self-denial of ... the Gospels is always the surrender of a lesser, dying self for a greater eternal one — the person God intended in creating you.... Jesus does not deny us personal fulfillment, but shows us the only true way to it. In him, we "find our life."[8]

- When you consider the recent opportunities you had to take up your cross (identified in question 3), how would you characterize the "lesser, dying self" and the "greater, eternal one" God wants to create in you?

How does it impact your perspective to think of your choices not as opportunities to *deny yourself* but as opportunities to *choose yourself* — to choose the kind of person you will become?

- Briefly identify a recent opportunity when you did choose to deny yourself. Looking back, in what ways would you say you found your life or became more of the person God intended as a result?

---

8. Dallas Willard, *Renovation of the Heart*, 68.

The Lost Soul

5. John used the Parable of the Soils (Matthew 13:3–9) to illustrate how we get to choose the state of our soul—and how we too often settle for living with a lost soul. The parable uses three kinds of soil as metaphors for the lost soul:

> *Hardened:* A soul that has surrounded itself with a protective shell and become cynical, bitter, and/or suspicious.
>
> *Rocky:* A soul that is shallow, preoccupied with its own needs, and seeks immediate gratification.
>
> *Thorny:* A soul that is cluttered, worried about externals (lifestyle, reputation, activities), and choked by desires for things besides God.

- All of us have experienced one or more of these soul conditions at some point. Of the three, which would you say is the one you tend to be most susceptible to?

- Whatever your susceptibility, it's unlikely that you intentionally set out to choose a hardened, shallow, or cluttered soul. So what is it you *did* set out to choose? For example, those who are susceptible to a hardened soul might say they set out to choose self-protection.

- In what ways, if any, would you say the choices you made involve self-deception? Or how have you tended to rationalize or justify your choices?

6. John said that soul language has to involve sin language — acknowledging both the wrong we do and the good we don't do.

- How would you describe the way you and others in your Christian community tend to talk about personal sin? For example, is it mostly avoided, spoken of plainly, or perhaps recast in terms such as brokenness or wounds?

- John described how sin splits the self. There were times when he had to keep two incompatible thoughts in his mind. One was, "I'm a good person." The other was, "I want to inflict pain." In what ways do you relate to John's statement? When are you most likely to experience a similar split in yourself?

- As John was coming to grips with painful truths about himself, Dallas put his hand on John's chest and prayed for the healing of his soul. What was your initial reaction to this story? Is this something you hope someone might do for you? Why or why not?

Souls in Community

7. At the end of the Session 1 group discussion, you had the opportunity to share what you need from the other group members and to write down the best ways you can be good companions to one another.

- Briefly restate what you asked for from the group in Session 1. What additions or clarifications would you like to make that would help the group know more about how to be a good companion to you? As each person responds, add any additional information to the Session 1 chart. (If you were absent from the last session, share your response to Session 1, question 7. Then use the chart to write down what is important to each member of the group.)

- In what ways, if any, did you find yourself responding differently to other members of the group in this session based on what they asked for in the previous session? What made that easy or difficult for you to do?

Individual Activity: What I Want to Remember (2 minutes)

Complete this activity on your own.

1. Briefly review the video outline and any notes you took.

2. In the space below, write down the most significant thing you gained in this session—from the teaching, activities, or discussions.

What I want to remember from this session . . .

Group Practice: Choosing the Condition of Your Soul

Every day we make choices that contribute to the condition of our soul and whether it will become hardened, rocky, thorny, or good soil.

The challenge we face as followers of Jesus is to consistently take up our cross—to choose self-denial for his sake. In this way, we develop a lifestyle of loving, sacrificial choices and exchange a "lesser, dying self" for a "greater, eternal one."

The group practice for this week is to become increasingly aware of your choices, and to be intentional in making loving, sacrificial choices.

- Each day, identify one relationship or circumstance as a focus for taking up your cross. Throughout the course of that day, your posture toward that person or circumstance should be one of making consistently loving, sacrificial choices. Keep in mind that choices include everything from subtle ("plausible deniability") choices to more obvious choices. Your choices also include the way you use your will, your mind, and your body. If possible, make your choices quietly and refrain from drawing too much attention to yourself. The goal overall is for these kinds of choices to become normal and routine.

- Set aside fifteen minutes at the beginning or end of the day to reflect on the previous twenty-four hours. How did you do? What loving, sacrificial choices did you make—or fail to make? How did your choices impact you? How did they impact the other person or circumstance? Briefly note your daily observations in a notepad or a journal.

- At the end of the week, review your daily notes. What stands out most to you about the ways in which you were able or unable to take up your cross through your choices? What did you discover about the condition of your soul?

Bring your notes from the week to the next group gathering. You'll have a chance to talk about your experiences and observations at the beginning of the Session 3 discussion.

Closing Prayer

Close your time together with prayer.

SESSION 2: Personal Study

Read and Learn

Read chapters 3–5 of the book *Soul Keeping*. Use the space below to note any insights or questions you want to bring to the next group session.

Study and Reflect

> The soul integrates the will and mind and body. Sin disintegrates them.
>
> *Soul Keeping*, page 58

1. We know our souls cannot function properly if sin is present, but it can be difficult to come to grips with the truth about ourselves. Often, that's because the sins we have the hardest time seeing are the ones that hide in plain sight. Author Dallas Willard described these as "normal" sins:

> The most spiritually dangerous things in me are the little habits of thought, feeling, and action that I regard as "normal," because "everyone is like that" and "it's only human."[9]

Use the prompts that follow to reflect on various areas of your life. What "little habits of thought, feeling, and action" do you regard as "normal," or justify with thoughts like "everyone is like that"? Consider areas of life such as your family relationships, body, pace of life, finances, social life, personal needs, work life, inner life, etc.

---

9. Dallas Willard, *The Divine Conspiracy*, 344.

My *habits of thought* ...
Example: *Why should I have to do that task? Nobody else is pitching in.*

My *habits of feeling* ...
Example: *I am completely justified in my anger. Anyone in my place would be angry.*

My *habits of action* ...
Example: *Everyone has debt. I'll charge it now and pay for it later.*

---

2. In addition to the sins we have a hard time seeing, we also have to contend with the deeper roots of sin and temptation — the failures we can never seem to overcome. The apostle Paul described his struggles this way:

> I know that nothing good lives in me, that is, in my sinful nature. I want to do what is right, but I can't. I want to do what is good, but I don't. I don't want to do what is wrong, but I do

it anyway. But if I do what I don't want to do, I am not really the one doing wrong; it is sin living in me that does it. I have discovered this principle of life — that when I want to do what is right, I inevitably do what is wrong. (Romans 7:18–21 NLT)

For a fresh perspective on this familiar passage, read it again from *The Message*:

If the power of sin within me keeps sabotaging my best intentions, I obviously need help! I realize that I don't have what it takes. I can will it, but I can't *do* it. I decide to do good, but I don't *really* do it; I decide not to do bad, but then I do it anyway. My decisions, such as they are, don't result in actions. Something has gone wrong deep within me and gets the better of me every time. It happens so regularly that it's predictable. The moment I decide to do good, sin is there to trip me up. (Romans 7:18–21 MSG)

What comes to mind when you think about the right or the good that you want to do but don't?

What is the wrong that gets the better of you every time — the thing or things you don't want to do but do anyway?

> This is what it means to lose your soul. It is not a cosmic threat. It is a clinical diagnosis. It is not "I could end up there." It is "I could become that."
>
> *Soul Keeping*, page 59

3. If losing your soul means, "I could become that," what "thats" might you identify in connection with your responses to questions 1 and 2? In other words, if these sins in your life continue unchecked, what could you become? How might your soul be at risk?

Conviction is not just the pain of getting caught or pain over consequences. It means a God-given, really sober sense of remorse over what I ought to feel remorseful about.... A prodigal son comes to his senses. The mighty King David is humbled by a phrase: "thou art the man." A sinful woman aching for forgiveness bathes Jesus' feet with her tears. In the same way the stomach hungers for food, the conscience hungers to be cleansed. It is a God-given ache for goodness.

Soul Keeping, pages 73–74

4. As you reflect on your responses to questions 1 and 2, where in your life are you most aware of a God-given ache for goodness?

What, specifically, is the goodness you want to experience?

> The soul, if it can only acknowledge its wounded condition, manifests amazing capacities for recovery when it finds its home in God and receives his grace.
>
> Dallas Willard, *Renovation of the Heart*, page 202

5. Read Psalm 32, a prayer of David that describes his experience of confession and forgiveness. Drawing on the psalm as a reference, use the space below to write your own prayer. Share the struggles you face and your discouragement over the sins that repeatedly trip you up. Confess anything for which you feel genuine remorse. Invite God to counsel you. Ask him to give you the desire and the power to do what pleases him. Thank him for his forgiveness — and rejoice in it!

WHAT THE SOUL NEEDS

*You must arrange your days so that you are experiencing
total contentment, joy, and confidence in your everyday life with God —
that and that alone is what makes a soul healthy.*

DALLAS WILLARD, QUOTED IN *SOUL KEEPING*

Group Discussion: Checking In (20 minutes)

A key part of getting to know God better is sharing your journey with others. Before watching the video, check in with each other about your experiences since the last session. For example:

- Briefly share your experience of the Session 2 group practice. What did you learn or experience in your daily times of choosing the condition of your soul by taking up your cross?

- What insights did you discover in the personal study or in the chapters you read from the book Soul Keeping?

- How did the last session impact your daily life or your relationship with God?

- What questions would you like to ask the other members of your group?

Video: What the Soul Needs (24 minutes)

Play the video segment for Session 3. As you watch, use the outline provided to follow along or to take additional notes on anything that stands out to you.

Notes

It is the nature of our soul to need — and it is part of our job as the soul's keeper to make sure those needs are being addressed.

Part of what it means to be human is to be limited in almost every way. There is one aspect of us that is utterly unlimited — it is the little thing known as desire. No matter what we have, we always want more.

All this desire is the soul crying out because it never has enough—and this is actually a really good thing.

The soul's infinite capacity to desire is the mirror image of God's infinite capacity to give.

The neediness of our soul is a pointer to God.

The unlimited neediness of the soul matches the unlimited grace of God. This is very good news that we sometimes turn bad by letting our soul's neediness point us to something *other* than God: money, power, career, hidden desires, substances (alcohol, cigarettes, unhealthy foods, etc.).

Our soul's problem is not its neediness, but its fallenness.

Instead of allowing our soul's need to serve as a pointer to God, we let it point us to other sources of ultimate devotion. This is what the Bible calls "idolatry."

Fainting is an indication of neediness—and there is something about the soul that longs to the point of fainting for God. The notion is that the soul cannot sustain itself.

"The main thing you will give to God is the person you become. . . . You, and nobody else, are responsible for the well-being of your soul" (Dallas Willard).

"You must arrange your days so that you are experiencing total contentment, joy, and confidence in your everyday life with God — that and that alone is what makes a soul healthy" (Dallas Willard).

The apostle Paul pointed out that you reap what you sow (Galatians 6:7). This is true with the soul.

We often live as though the law of consequences doesn't actually apply to us. Our capacity to live in denial about this is deeply damaging to the soul.

The solution is quite simple, but also very hard to do:

Slow down.

Look up.

Lean in.

Listen to God.

Be responsible for faithfully keeping [y]our soul.

And it's an all-day, everyday deal.

"That person is like a tree planted by streams of water, which yields its fruit in season and whose leaf does not wither—whatever they do prospers" (Psalm 1:3).

Our soul is like an inner stream of water that gives strength, direction, and harmony to every area of our life. This is a deep image from the Scriptures.

At the heart of Jesus' teachings are these truths:

Make room in your life to care for your soul.

Protect it. Guard it. Keep it.

Only one person can keep the soul—and that one person is *you*.

Five indicators of sinkhole syndrome

1. A soul without a center has difficulty making a decision.

   A centered soul is able to resist temptation and make the sacrifices that are worth making.

2. A soul without a center feels constantly vulnerable to people or circumstances.

   A centered soul takes refuge in God (Psalm 57:1).

3. A soul without a center lacks patience.

   A centered soul is at rest.

4. A soul without a center is easily thrown.

   A centered soul can hang on easily.

5. A soul without a center finds its identity in externals.

   A soul centered in God always knows it has a heavenly Father who will hold its anxiety, fear, and pain.

This is life: to place my soul every moment in the presence and care of God.

The soul cannot meet its central needs by itself. It requires care.

Group Discussion (44 minutes)

Take a few minutes to talk about what you just watched.

1. What part of the teaching had the most impact on you?

Your Soul Is "Bob"

2. John likened the soul to the title character in the movie *What About Bob?* Like Bob, he said, the soul cries out: "Gimme! Gimme! Gimme! I need! I need! I need!"

- How do you respond to the idea that your soul is needy? For example, is it an idea that resonates with you and makes sense of your experience? Do you have trouble relating to it, or feel resistant to it for some reason? Share the reasons for your response.

- In the movie, Bob's doctor (played by Richard Dreyfuss) is frustrated and annoyed by Bob's constant demands and neediness—at first he puts Bob off, then tries to lose him, and ultimately attempts to kill him. In what ways, if any, have you responded similarly in the face of your own neediness—with annoyance or perhaps by trying to diminish, avoid, or deny it? What happens as a result?

Desiring God

3. The neediness of the soul—its capacity for unlimited desire—is a good thing when it points us toward God. Jesus told two stories that characterize the soul whose desire is directed to God:

> The Kingdom of Heaven is like a treasure that a man discovered hidden in a field. In his excitement, he hid it again and sold everything he owned to get enough money to buy the field.
>
> Again, the Kingdom of Heaven is like a merchant on the lookout for choice pearls. When he discovered a pearl of great value, he sold everything he owned and bought it! (Matthew 13:44–46 NLT)

- Put yourself in the place of the characters in both stories and try to imagine their thoughts and emotions. What three to five words or phrases would you use to describe them?

- Both men sold everything they owned—and not grudgingly or fearfully but eagerly. Why? What parallels would you expect to find in the God-directed soul?

- When would you say you have felt most aware of this kind of need or eager desire for God? (For example, in a season of spiritual hunger or seeking.) If you can, try to distinguish your desire for God from a desire for God's gifts or provision.

- Overall, how would you characterize the degree of your desire for God right now? Is it on the high side, low side, or somewhere between? Share the reasons for your response.

4. The soul's capacity for desire becomes a bad thing only when we allow it to point us to something other than God. This is what the Bible calls idolatry. John defined idolatry as "the sin of the soul meeting its needs with anything that distances it from God." He also said we commit this kind of idolatry every day.

- How do you respond to the idea that we commit this kind of idolatry every day? Is it something that feels true to you—both about yourself and other Christians you know? Share the reasons for your response.

- In your own life, how do you recognize when something has moved from being a legitimate desire into the idolatry zone?

- We can't turn away from idols with sheer willpower; instead, we have to turn toward something else. How would you describe the difference between turning away from a personal idol with sheer willpower, and turning your soul and its needs toward God? What actions would you take—or refrain from taking—in both cases?

You Must Arrange Your Days

5. When John was at a needy point in his soul and asked for guidance, his friend Dallas said, "You must arrange your days so you are experiencing deep contentment, joy, and confidence in your everyday life with God."

- We all arrange our days around something important to us—our families, jobs, and personal interests. What would you say are the top one or two things around which you routinely arrange your days?

- What kinds of things might have to change if you were to rearrange your days around "experiencing deep contentment, joy, and confidence in your everyday life with God"?

- Of the three things Dallas listed—contentment, joy, and confidence—which would you say you need most in your relationship with God right now?

Souls in Community

6. Take a few moments to reflect on what you've learned and experienced together in this study so far.

   - How has learning more about the soul impacted you and your relationship with God?

   - Since the first session, what shifts have you noticed in yourself in terms of how you relate to the group? For example, do you feel more or less guarded, understood, challenged, encouraged, connected, etc.?

• What adjustments, if any, would you like to make to the Session 1 chart that would help other members of the group know how to be better companions for you?

Individual Activity: What I Want to Remember (2 minutes)

Complete this activity on your own.

1. Briefly review the video outline and any notes you took.

2. In the space below, write down the most significant thing you gained in this session—from the teaching, activities, or discussions.

   What I want to remember from this session . . .

Group Practice: Addressing Your Soul

Normally when we are angry or frustrated, we beat up on ourselves or, worse, on others. We may find temporary relief from that, but the soul still cries for attention. John shared an example of how he paid attention to his soul once when he was angry: "I just stopped and asked myself, 'Why are you angry, O my soul?'" Addressing his soul directly reminded him that he lived in God's presence. He began to pray and felt his soul being freed as he talked to God about his anger.

The group practice this week is to use your emotional reactions as a prompt to engage your soul in prayerful conversation.

- Like the psalmist, you might use the occasion of discouragement or frustration as a prompt to address your soul: "Why are you down in the dumps, dear soul? Why are you crying the blues?" (Psalm 43:5 MSG). Or it may be that joy over God's goodness becomes an occasion to pay attention to your soul: "O my soul, bless God, don't forget a single blessing!" (Psalm 103:2 MSG).

- Converse with your soul as if it were another person. Ask questions, seek understanding. Invite God into the conversation and listen for what he might say to you.

- Set aside fifteen minutes at the beginning or end of each day to reflect on the previous twenty-four hours. What was it like to have conversations with your soul? What, if anything, would you change about your practice for tomorrow? Note your daily observations on a pad of paper or in a journal.

- At the end of the week, review your daily notes. What stands out most to you about your experiences of giving attention to your soul in this way?

Bring your notes from the week to the next group gathering. You'll have a chance to talk about your experiences and observations at the beginning of the Session 4 discussion.

Closing Prayer

Close your time together with prayer.

SESSION 3: Personal Study

Read and Learn

Read chapters 6–8 of the book *Soul Keeping*. Use the space below to note any insights or questions you want to bring to the next group session.

Study and Reflect

> Anytime I sin, I am allowing some competing desire to have higher priority than God and God's will for my life. That means that in that moment I have put something on a pedestal higher than God. That something is my idol. All sin involves idolatry.
>
> *Soul Keeping*, pages 78–79

1. Many Christians love God and want to follow him more closely, but one thing or another always seems to get in the way. This "one thing" is the true devotion of the soul. To get an idea of what this looks like, read "The Soul's True Devotion" in the sidebar that follows. Then respond to these questions:

What comes to mind when you think of what your "one thing" might be — that something that always seems to get in the way of following Christ?

How, specifically, have you put this issue or behavior on a pedestal recently? Briefly identify two or three examples.

The Soul's True Devotion

Most people, especially religious people, would probably say their souls are devoted to God or a higher calling or an ideal. We want to believe that's true even as we devote our souls to something else. Consider as honestly as possible the following statements. If any of them even slightly resemble your thoughts, it is quite possible you have discovered the true devotion of your soul:

- I think about money a lot, as in getting more of it. Sometimes I fantasize about winning the lottery or coming into a big inheritance. I have a mental wish list of the things I'd like to buy if money were no object.

- I wish I had more power and control over others. It seems as if my spouse and kids just don't respect me enough. Ditto at work. I know I would handle it carefully—I would just like to be a more powerful person.

- I have missed important family events in order to pursue my career. I justify it by telling myself and my family that this is what it takes to provide for them. I tell myself that if I keep working hard, I will reach a level where I will be able to relax a little and spend more time with the people I love.

(cont.)

- I consider myself an honest person, someone with good values. But I would set those values aside to pursue something important to me if I knew no one else would know about it.

- I have desires that I prefer not to have my spouse know about. If I am confronted by any of those desires, I become defensive and try to justify it.

- I have secrets that I am willing to lie to protect.

- More than once I have had arguments over something I wanted to do but my spouse did not want to do. Or over something I wanted to buy that my spouse didn't think I should buy.

- Aside from my family and others I love, there are things in my life that if they were lost or destroyed, it would crush me, devastate me.

- If my doctor told me I had to give up (alcohol, cigarettes, red meat, salt/sodium, sugar, caffeine, etc.) because it was seriously putting my health at risk, I would find it difficult to the point of being impossible. I likely would not tell anyone in order to avoid accountability.

- If you asked my family what was most important to me, they would likely refer to my job, my favorite hobby, making money.... They would probably not say it was them.

- I love God, and I want to more closely follow him, but there is one thing that always seems to get in the way, and it's _____.

Soul Keeping, pages 79–80

Your soul is vulnerable because it is needy. If you meet those needs with the wrong things, game over. Or at least, game not going well.

Soul Keeping, page 77

---

2. Keeping in mind the neediness of your soul, how would you describe the legitimate needs behind the "one thing" you identified in question 1? For example, behind a devotion to success and career advancement might be a need for significance and affirmation; behind a devotion to money might be a need for security or freedom; behind a devotion to an addictive substance might be a need for comfort or relief from pain.

---

3. The apostle Peter used the image of combat to describe the damage that indulging misguided desires has on us — these desires "wage war against your very souls" (1 Peter 2:11 NLT). Dallas Willard explains how this happens:

> How do fleshly lusts war against the soul? Very simply, by enticing us to uproot our dependent life, pulling it away from God, which will deprive our soul of what it needs to function correctly in the enlivening and regulation of our whole being. To allow lust (or strong desires) to govern our life is to exalt our will over God's.[10]

In what ways might the issue you identified in question 1 be waging war on your soul, enticing you to uproot your dependence on God?

---

10. Dallas Willard, *Renovation of the Heart*, 210.

What fears or concerns come to mind when you think about what it would mean to remain dependent on God for what you need in this area of your life?

> This is what we might call Reality 101 when it comes to the soul. It is the law of consequences. Paul put it like this: "You reap what you sow." ... Mostly we like to say that as a warning to other people. Apparently we believe that by some magic, the law of consequences doesn't apply to us.
>
> *Soul Keeping*, page 86

4. Our capacity to live in denial about the law of consequences is vast and deeply damaging to the soul. For example:

I can spend without getting into debt.

I can lie without getting caught.

I can let my temper fly without damaging my relationships.

I can have a bad attitude at work and get away with it.

I can neglect the Bible and still know God.

What similar statements might you use to describe the denial associated with the issue you identified in question 1?

What consequences, if any, would you say you are already experiencing?

---

5. Read Psalm 106, which describes how the Israelites repeatedly uprooted their dependence on God—by forgetting God's miracles and kindnesses, turning to idols or their own cravings, and refusing to believe his promises. Use the psalm as the basis for writing your own prayer. Acknowledge the ways you have pulled away from God and sought to meet your needs on your own terms. Share your fears and concerns about depending on him to meet these needs. Humbly entrust yourself to his care.

forgeting God's works
fear that He can't/won't
provide
jealous of leaders
idols
despising God's blessings
grumbling
disobedience
worshipped other God's
rebellious

THE PRACTICE OF GRACE

The greatest saints are not those who need less grace, but those who consume the most grace, who indeed are most in need of grace — those who are saturated by grace in every dimension of their being. Grace to them is like breath.

DALLAS WILLARD, *RENOVATION OF THE HEART*

Group Discussion: Checking In (20 minutes)

A key part of getting to know God better is sharing your journey with others. Before watching the video, check in with each other about your experiences since the last session. For example:

- Briefly share your experience of the Session 3 group practice. What did you learn or experience in your daily times of addressing your soul?
- What insights did you discover in the personal study or in the chapters you read from the book *Soul Keeping*?
- How did the last session impact your daily life or your relationship with God?
- What questions would you like to ask the other members of your group?

Video: The Practice of Grace (22 minutes)

Play the video segment for Session 4. As you watch, use the outline provided to follow along or to take additional notes on anything that stands out to you.

Notes

Jesus faced enormous stresses, difficulties, and pain. Yet he never got sarcastic, cynical, unloving, or burned out. No one took away his joy.

Jesus lived in a divine rhythm where grace was constantly flowing into him. And then from him, grace was constantly flowing out.

There are four stages in the cycle of grace.

1. Acceptance

For Jesus, acceptance and identity come before ministry and achievement.

There is no one you need to impress because you have already been accepted by God.

2. Sustenance

The soul was designed to run on God's grace.

For your soul to be well, it needs to be *with* God.

The "with God" life is a life of inward peace and contentment. Wherever you are, you can be aware of God in this moment.

3. Significance

Our lives were meant to be signs that point beyond ourselves to God. That's why we are not just selves, we're souls.

Jesus communicated to people that significance is a gift, not an achievement.

A rested soul is the secret to what Jesus called the easy yoke.

4. Achievement

"I am the vine; you are the branches. If you remain in me and I in you, you will bear much fruit; apart from me you can do nothing" (John 15:5).

What we really have to learn is how to live in grace with God each moment. That's what it means to abide in the vine—to live intimately with Jesus from one moment to the next.

The Cycle of Grace vs. the Cycle of Works

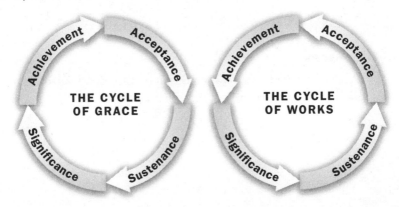

When the soul and the grace of God occupy the throne of your life:
    Your *will* is undivided and obeys God with joy.
    Your *mind* thinks thoughts of truth and beauty.
    Your *body* is filled with appetites that lead to excellent living.
    Your *soul* desires what is wholesome and good.

"A woman giving birth to a child has pain because her time has come; but when her baby is born she forgets the anguish because of her joy that a child is born into the world. So with you: Now is your time of grief, but I will see you again and you will rejoice, and no one will take away your joy" (John 16:21–22).

There will be great pain, and there will be great joy. In the end, joy wins. So if joy has not yet won, it is not yet the end.

Joy wins. That's the promise.

We will be forever alive. This is what the soul craves. This is grace.

Group Discussion   (46 minutes)

Take time to talk about what you just watched.

1. What part of the teaching had the most impact on you?

The Flow of Grace

2. John described Jesus as living in a divine rhythm where grace was constantly flowing into him, and then constantly flowing out from him. Overall, how would you describe your experience of grace over the course of your journey with God? For example, has it been a steady flow of grace? An occasional shower of grace? An "eddy," where grace flows in but doesn't flow out? A gush at the beginning and a trickle ever since?

3. Dallas Willard describes the role of grace in the life of the believer this way:

> To "grow in grace" means to utilize more and more grace to live by, until everything we do is assisted by grace. Then, whatever we do in word or deed will all be done in the name of the Lord Jesus (Colossians 3:17). The greatest saints are not those who need *less* grace, but those who consume the most grace, who indeed are most in need of grace—those who are saturated by grace in every dimension of their being. Grace to them is like breath.[11]

---

11. Dallas Willard, *Renovation of the Heart*, 93.

- We know we are saved by grace and that we need grace for our failures and challenges, but Dallas points out how we need grace for everything, and even greater amounts of it as we grow. If we primarily associate our need for grace with sin and hardships, how might this perspective impact both our understanding of grace and our ability to *grow* in grace?

- Take a deep breath in and let it out slowly. If grace is like breath, what insights or parallels might you draw between this simple act of breathing and what it means to live in a cycle of grace?

The Cycle of Grace

4. **Acceptance.** Briefly review the diagrams in the video notes section that contrast the Cycle of Grace with the Cycle of Works. One begins with acceptance and one ends with acceptance. Which diagram would you say best characterizes your life right now? Share the reasons for your response.

5. **Sustenance.** For the soul to be well, it needs to be with God. This is sustaining grace—grace that replenishes and enables the soul to rest. John described Dallas as the personification of a soul sustained in grace. He seemed to always be aware of God's presence. And no matter what he was doing—sharing a meal, having a conversation, going for a walk—Dallas never rushed. These things made Dallas a healing presence.

   • Who do you know that you would describe as a healing presence or as a soul sustained in grace? What two or three key characteristics make you feel like it is healing to be with them?

   • On the video, John acknowledged that he wondered about himself, "Is it healing to be with me?" Then he asked, "Is it a healing thing to be with you?" What was your initial response when John posed the question?

   • The key to the "with God" life is not more church activities or devotional practices or trying harder to be good. It's allowing God to make every moment of our lives glorious with his presence. Imagine for a moment that Jesus is physically present with you right now. In what ways would this moment be different? In what ways would you be different?

6. Significance. Dallas Willard writes, "We are built to count, as water is made to run downhill. We are placed in a specific context to count in ways no one else does. That is our destiny."[12] We tend to think that we "count" because of what we do. Our contributions do have value but our significance is a gift.

- Briefly think back over the last few days. What experiences did you have that made you feel significant, even in a small way? Overall, would you say these experiences were based more on what you did or on who you are?

- One way to think about your significance—how you "count in ways no one else does"—is to consider what people might say about you at your funeral. Aside from acknowledging your accomplishments, what kinds of things do you think the people in your life might say about you and why you were significant to them?

---

12. Dallas Willard, *The Divine Conspiracy*, 15.

7. Achievement. Achievement is how the grace that has flowed into us — through acceptance, sustenance, and significance — now flows out of us. It is the fruit we bear for God and his kingdom. In order to bear fruit, we have to abide in Christ:

> I am the vine; you are the branches. If you remain in me and I in you, you will bear much fruit; apart from me you can do nothing. (John 15:5)

This requirement to abide is one that Christ also claimed for himself:

> I tell you the truth, the Son can do nothing by himself. He does only what he sees the Father doing. Whatever the Father does, the Son also does.... I can do nothing on my own. (John 5:19, 30 NLT)

- How does it influence your understanding of achievement to think of it as grace flowing out of you?

- What would you say is the most fruitful aspect of your life right now?

- To abide in Christ requires dependence on him—to attempt nothing *independent* of him. How do you recognize this dependence on Christ in connection with the fruitfulness you just described?

Souls in Community

8. Take a moment to touch base with each other about how you're doing in the group. Use one of the sentence starters below, or your own statement, to help the group learn more about how to be a good companion to you.

I want to give you permission to challenge me more about . . .

An area where I really need your help or sensitivity is . . .

It always helps me to feel more connected to the group when . . .

Something I've learned about myself because of this group is . . .

Individual Activity: What I Want to Remember (2 minutes)

Complete this activity on your own.

1. Briefly review the video outline and any notes you took.

2. In the space below, write down the most significant thing you gained in this session—from the teaching, activities, or discussions.

What I want to remember from this session . . .

Group Practice: Practicing the Presence of God

A key part of what John described as the "with God" life is practicing the presence of God. We do this by directing and then redirecting our minds to God throughout the day (Isaiah 26:3; Colossians 3:2). And as we are intentional in keeping God before us, Dallas Willard says, "Soon our minds will return to God as the needle of a compass constantly returns to the north."[13]

Here is how Brother Lawrence, a seventeenth-century French monk, described what it means to continually direct our minds to God:

> He requires not great matters of us; a little remembrance of him from time to time; a little adoration; sometimes to pray for his grace; sometimes to offer him your sufferings, sometimes to return him thanks for the favors he has given you, and still gives you, in the midst of your troubles, and to console yourself with him as often as you can. Lift up your heart to him, sometimes even at your meals, and when you are in company: the least little remembrance will

---

13. Dallas Willard, *The Great Omission* (San Francisco: HarperSanFrancisco, 2006), 125.

always be acceptable to him. You need not cry very loudly; he is nearer to us than we are aware of.[14]

The group practice this week is to practice the presence of God—to begin each day with this challenge: *How many moments of my life today can I fill with conscious awareness of and surrender to God's presence?*

- Before you go to bed at night or as you get ready in the morning, imagine what it would be like to do each part of the day ahead in God's presence. At home, at work, commuting, running errands, surfing the Web, watching the news, being with others—how might you do each part of your day *with an awareness of* God?

- Throughout the day, keep directing and redirecting your mind to God. If you find it helpful, write something like "practice the presence," "God wants to be with me now," or a favorite Scripture verse on Post-It notes and place them strategically around your home, your workplace, and in your car. Don't be discouraged if you find it difficult, especially at first. As Brother Lawrence affirms, every little remembrance pleases God. God is happy for you to start where you are and grow from there.

- Set aside fifteen minutes at the beginning or end of each day to reflect on the previous twenty-four hours. How did you do at practicing, or failing to practice, the presence of God? Note your daily observations on a pad of paper or in a journal.

- At the end of the week, review your daily notes. What stands out most to you about your experiences of practicing the presence of God?

Bring your notes from the week to the next group gathering. You'll have a chance to talk about your experiences and observations at the beginning of the Session 5 discussion.

Closing Prayer

Close your time together with prayer.

---

14. Brother Lawrence, *The Practice of the Presence of God* (Benton, AR: Benton Press, 2013), 28.

SESSION 4: Personal Study

Read and Learn

Read chapters 9–11 of the book *Soul Keeping*. Use the space below to note any insights or questions you want to bring to the next group session.

Study and Reflect

> Jesus began this grand experiment with his twelve followers. They're like his pilot group. He appointed those twelve disciples so that they might be with him.
>
> *Soul Keeping*, page 114

---

1. Frank Laubach (1884–1970) was a Christian missionary and author who devoted his life to addressing issues of poverty, injustice, and illiteracy in the Philippines and the United States. One of his best-known writings was a pamphlet called "The Game with Minutes." In it, he challenged Christians to keep God in mind for one second of every minute throughout the day. He considered the "with God" life one of God's great experiments:

> The most wonderful discovery that has ever come to me is that I do not have to wait until some future time for the glorious hour.... *This hour* can be heaven. Any hour for *any* body can be as rich as God! For do you not see that God is trying experiments

with human lives. That is why there are so many of them. He has [seven billion] experiments going around the world at this moment. And his question is, "How far will this man and that woman allow me to carry this hour?"[15]

How did you find yourself responding to Laubach's assertions about the reality of God's presence, that *"This hour* can be heaven"? For example, does it excite you, leave you cold, make you think it's nice for some people but not possible for you?

When scientists conduct experiments, they assume some trial and error. It's all part of the process of how they make discoveries. If your life is part of God's experiment, how would you describe your trials and errors? In other words, what discoveries have you made about living in God's presence?

15. Frank C. Laubach, *Letters by a Modern Mystic* (Colorado Springs: Purposeful Designs Publications, 1955, 2007), 14.

2. In any experiment, you start by forming a hypothesis. A hypothesis is basically an assumption that you test by putting it to work, often in a laboratory. Your laboratory is your life—that's where you play out your experiment. When it comes to the soul's life with God, there are three assumptions to put to the test:

(a) *God wants to make every moment of my life glorious with his presence.*

(b) *The best place to start doing life with God is in small moments.*

(c) *People will look different when I see them with God.*

Use the prompts that follow to reflect on each of the three hypotheses.

(a) God wants to make every moment of my life glorious with his presence.

> I have set the LORD always before me. (Psalm 16:8a ESV)

> We take captive every thought to make it obedient to Christ. (2 Corinthians 10:5b)

These verses speak to the need for our souls to be completely and thoroughly with God. But it does not happen automatically. "Set" and "take captive" are active verbs, implying that you have a role in cultivating an awareness of God's presence.

In the course of an ordinary day, how often would you say you are aware of or actively cultivating God's presence?

☐ Almost never

☐ Occasionally

☐ About half the time

☐ Much of the time

☐ Almost always

Overall, how have you tended to think about what it means to experience an awareness of God's presence? For example, do you tend to think it just "happens," that it happens mostly in such settings as church or nature, or that God is present when you pray, etc.?

Read the personal story John Ortberg shares in the following sidebar "Setting the Mind on God." Using this practical example as a reference, in what ways do you sense God may be inviting you to join his experiment — to actively cultivate an awareness of his presence?

In what areas of life or in what relationships do you especially need an awareness of God's presence?

Setting the Mind on God

I was invited to speak in the chapel of the Naval Academy. It's an old, historic, marble, beautiful building. I looked out at the front couple of rows, and there are a bunch of young midshipmen all dressed up in their uniforms. They have devoted their lives to try to serve our country. In that moment I set my thoughts on God, even breathing a silent prayer: "God, I'm so grateful to be here. I'm so grateful there are young people who commit their lives to that." In that moment, I had chosen to set my thoughts on God.

Before I was introduced, the leader of this service announced the person who was going to be speaking at the next Navy chapel. I knew that person and allowed myself to think, "I wish that guy wasn't coming here to speak because he'll give a better talk than me. People will like his talk more than they'll like my talk." This is how quickly we can set our thoughts back on ourselves. But here's the best part of this experiment of seeing how much of each day we can meet the need of our souls to be with God. As soon as I became aware of my self-centeredness, I surrendered my thoughts back to God and enjoyed his presence again. That's just how God works with us—he relentlessly pursues us because all he has ever wanted is to be with us. He reaches out to slaves, people in prison, and people like me doing silly, foolish things and says, "Welcome back."

Soul Keeping, pages 118–119

(b) The best place to start doing life with God is in small moments.

> Do not despise these small beginnings, for the LORD rejoices
> to see the work begin. (Zechariah 4:10a NLT)

The "work" this verse refers to is the rebuilding of the temple,
God's dwelling place. The focus of God's joy is not on the grandeur
of the completed building but on its humble beginnings.

Where in your life with God are you holding back because you
think only grand gestures or big changes "count"?

Read the personal story John Ortberg shares in the following sidebar "Beginning with Small Moments." His example may seem like a
very small thing, but that's the point! As part of your participation
in God's experiment, what small step might you take in connection
with the area of life you identified?

Beginning with Small Moments

Hurry is one of the major barriers that keeps me from life on the vine. So I have developed all these little tricks to get me through airports as quickly as possible. When I'm getting off a plane, I usually have a computer bag and a suitcase with wheels. The aisles are really narrow, so I hold the computer bag and the suitcase in either hand while I'm going down the aisle. Then when I get into that broader walkway I put the suitcase down, raise the handle, and put the long strap on the computer bag over it so I can wheel the whole thing out easily. Here is the problem. When I'm doing that, if I pull over to the side of the walkway, people behind pass me — I feel like they're beating me. Can't let that happen. So as I raise the handle on my suitcase, I sort of swing it around so that it's blocking the walkway, preventing some little old lady or sales rep from passing me. I'm not proud of this.

I was executing this blocking move a few weeks ago when I heard this little whisper: "John, let someone pass you. You're just not that important. I don't need you to hurry, plus it makes you obnoxious to other people. So today, pull over to the side, take a breath, assemble your little luggage cart, and let someone pass you."

I have learned to listen to that still small voice. I did as I was told. I stepped to the side, assembled my bags, and watched three people pass me, and it actually felt good. It felt good to not be in such a hurry. It felt even better to recognize that God was with me. In that small moment. As the rest of the world rushed by.

Sometimes a jetway can become a cathedral.

Soul Keeping, pages 119–120

(c) People will look different when I see them with God.

> From now on we regard no one from a worldly point of view.
> (2 Corinthians 5:16)

The larger context for the apostle Paul's statement is reconciliation. Just as God reconciled the world to himself through Christ, Christ has entrusted his followers with the message and the ministry of reconciliation (2 Corinthians 5:18–19).

What relationship comes to mind when you consider those you tend to regard from a worldly point of view? (A worldly point of view might be based on such things as someone's role, social standing, ethnicity, career, education, finances, physical appearance, or any other external characteristic.) Consider individuals as well as groups of people.

Read the example John Ortberg shares in the following sidebar "Looking at People Differently." How does it influence your view of the individual or group you identified to think of God looking at them at the same time you are looking at them?

In what ways do you sense God may be inviting you to join his experiment in connection with this person or group?

Looking at People Differently

When we are living with God, we will see people as God sees them. If I'm aware God is here with me, and God is looking at you at the same moment I'm looking at you, it will change how I respond to you. Instead of seeing you as the annoying server at McDonald's who messed up my order, I will see you as someone God loved enough to send his Son to die on your behalf. I will see you as a real person who got up dreading going to work, dealing with impatient customers, being on her feet all day. In other words, I will no longer see you as everyone else sees you.... From now on, now that my soul is centered with God in Jesus, I won't look at people the same way.

Soul Keeping, page 120

---

3. Read Psalm 139:1 – 18 which praises God for his intimate presence in our lives. Drawing on the psalm as a reference, use the space below to write your own prayer. Invite God into the areas of life where you struggle to set your mind on him. Ask him to give you joy and a sense of expectancy as you begin to experiment with practicing his presence each day. Praise him for his constant and loving presence.

THE PRACTICE
OF GRATITUDE

God has yet to bless anyone
except where they actually are.
It is here we can be grateful.

DALLAS WILLARD

Group Discussion: Checking In (20 minutes)

A key part of getting to know God better is sharing your journey with others. Before watching the video, check in with each other about your experiences since the last session. For example:

- Briefly share your experience of the Session 4 group practice. What did you learn or experience from practicing the presence of God?

- What insights did you discover in the personal study or in the chapters you read from the book *Soul Keeping*?

- How did the last session impact your daily life or your relationship with God?

- What questions would you like to ask the other members of your group?

Video: The Practice of Gratitude (22 minutes)

Play the video segment for Session 5. As you watch, use the outline provided to follow along or to take additional notes on anything that stands out to you.

Notes

The Hebrew term for "gratitude" literally means "recognizing the good."

There are always bad things vying for our attention, but you can say, "I choose to recognize the good." That's what sustains the soul.

"Let the message of Christ dwell among you richly as you teach and admonish one another with all wisdom through psalms, hymns, and songs from the Spirit, singing to God with gratitude in your hearts. And whatever you do, whether in word or deed, do it all in the name of the Lord Jesus, giving thanks to God the Father through him" (Colossians 3:16 – 17).

The soul needs freedom.

The soul cries out to be free, but the common perception is that Christianity stands in the way of freedom.

There are two kinds of freedom:

- Freedom *from*, which is freedom from external constraints
- Freedom *for*, which is about living the kind of life I was made to live

Our culture doesn't crave freedom *for*; it craves freedom *from*. Eventually you'll discover that only freedom *for* can set you free.

The soul is what integrates all of the parts of a person into a whole. The only way for the soul to be free is for all the parts of our personhood to be rightly ordered, rightly connected.

"I will always obey your law, for ever and ever. I will walk about in freedom, for I have sought out your precepts" (Psalm 119:44–45).

As we follow God's will and God's ways, and receive power for our souls to be healed and integrated, we are freed.

The soul needs blessing.

"There are two great words in the Bible that describe the posture of our souls toward other people. One is *bless*. The other is *curse*" (Dallas Willard).

Blessing is the projection of good into the life of another. It is an overt act of our will.

"The LORD bless you and keep you; the LORD make His face shine upon you, and be gracious to you; the LORD lift up His countenance upon you, and give you peace" (Numbers 6:24–26 NKJV).

How to bless:

- Blessing takes time, so don't hurry.

- Turn to the one you want to bless and look him or her in the eyes. Allow your mind to focus on the person before you.

- "The Lord bless you." This means, "May the Lord constantly bring good into your life."

- "The Lord keep you." This means we are asking God to protect this person, and that the sacrificial love of Christ guard all that is sacred and precious about them.

- "The Lord make his face shine upon you." Picture a grandparent doting on a grandchild. Glory was meant to be shared.

- "The Lord lift up his countenance upon you." We ask God to let his presence be fully known.

- "The Lord give you peace." This is what we want for those we love—for them to experience unthreatened, undisturbed, life-giving peace.

We have the ability not just to bless others, but to bless God. The grateful soul loves blessing God.

Back in Jesus' day, every devout Israelite would pray what was called the Eighteen Benedictions. A "bene-diction" literally means "good word." In Hebrew, a benediction was any prayer that began with the word "bless."

Blessed are you, Lord, who abundantly forgives.

Blessed are you, Lord, who heals the sick.

Blessed are you, Lord, who blesses the years.

Blessed are you, Lord, who loves righteousness and justice.

You will not always feel grateful. But you can take the time each day to remember your benefits, see your benefactor, and thank him for his blessings.

Gratitude can be the posture of our soul.

Group Discussion (44 minutes)

Take time to talk about what you just watched.

1. What part of the teaching had the most impact on you?

Gratitude

2. The Hebrew word for "gratitude" is *hikarat hatov,* which means "recognizing the good." In the course of your everyday life, how would you rate yourself on your ability to consistently recognize the good (regardless of circumstances)? Circle the number on the continuum that best describes your response.

1	2	3	4	5	6	7	8	9	10

I very rarely recognize the good or feel genuinely grateful.

I can always recognize the good and find something to be genuinely grateful for.

If you feel comfortable, share the number you circled. Overall, would you say you tend to be more likely or less likely than other people to recognize the good? Share any examples you can recall to illustrate your response.

Freedom

3. One of the benefits of a consistent posture of gratitude is freedom. John described two kinds of freedom: freedom *from*, which means being without external constraints; and freedom *for*, which means living the kind of life we were made to live.

   • If you could choose freedom *from* in any area of your life right now, what would it be? What external constraints do you wish you could be rid of?

   • Similarly, if you could choose freedom *for* in any area of your life, what would it be? In other words, where do you feel you lack the freedom to become the person you want to be?

4. We tend to associate threats to our freedom with external constraints, but the threats to soul freedom often have an internal rather than an external source. They come from unaddressed brokenness, weakness, dividedness, or sin. For example:

   You want to stop drinking, but you can't.

   You want to live with a happy, cheerful, optimistic attitude, but you don't.

   You want to quit yelling at your kids, but you can't.

   You want to be the kind of person who manages anger well, but you aren't.

   You'd like to think you have become unselfish, but you haven't.

The apostle Paul describes his experience of internal threats this way:

> I don't really understand myself, for I want to do what is right, but I don't do it. Instead, I do what I hate.... I have discovered this principle of life — that when I want to do what is right, I inevitably do what is wrong. I love God's law with all my heart. But there is another power within me that is at war with my mind. This power makes me a slave to the sin that is still within me. Oh, what a miserable person I am! (Romans 7:15, 21 – 24 NLT)

- Paul describes his condition as "miserable." When you consider how your lack of internal freedom impacts you, what three words or phrases would you use to describe it?

- John stated that the only way to achieve soul freedom is to surrender. We must acknowledge that there is a spiritual order that God has designed *for* us. Given the misery we experience when our souls are not free, why do you think it is so hard for most of us to surrender? If you feel comfortable, share any personal experiences that illustrate your response.

Partner Activity: Blessing

5. When we feed our souls gratitude by consistently recognizing the good, we become capable of bestowing blessing. Blessing is the projection of good into the life of another. This activity provides an opportunity for you to experience what it's like to both give and receive a blessing. Read through the directions as a group before breaking up into pairs.

Directions

- Pair up with one other person.

- One person gives the blessing and the other person receives the blessing. The receiver may want to set down his or her book and any other study materials. The one giving the blessing should give it without hurrying. Glance at the text of the blessing one line at a time, and then look the receiver in the eyes as you say each line:

  > The LORD bless you and keep you;
  > The LORD make his face shine upon you,
  > And be gracious to you;
  > The LORD lift up his countenance upon you,
  > And give you peace.

- Allow a moment of quiet after the blessing to let the words sink in.

- Then switch roles and repeat the blessing process.

- If you are done before others in the group, wait quietly until everyone has had a chance to finish giving and receiving a blessing. Then come back together as a group to continue your discussion.

6. Discuss your experience of giving and receiving a blessing.

- What was it like to *give* the blessing? For example, did you find it easier or harder than you had anticipated? What thoughts or emotions were you aware of in yourself as you gave the blessing?

- What was it like to *receive* the blessing? What made it easy or difficult for you to receive it and really take it in?

- The blessing conveys God's *protection*, *glory*, *presence*, and *peace* to the receiver. Which of these things were you most aware of needing from God as you received the blessing? In what ways, if any, did you receive what you needed through the blessing?

- Based on your experience, is this way of giving and receiving blessing something you'd like to do again? Share the reasons for your response.

Souls in Community

7. At the end of each session, you've had the opportunity to spend some time talking about your connections within the group, and especially about how to be good companions to one another.

- What are your observations about this portion of the discussion? For example, what, if any, differences do you notice in yourself and in the group when you are talking about yourself in relationship to the group (rather than about the content of the curriculum or your other relationships)?

- Do you tend to look forward to this portion of the discussion or do you find yourself wishing you could avoid it? Why?

Individual Activity: What I Want to Remember (2 minutes)

Complete this activity on your own.

1. Briefly review the video outline and any notes you took.

2. In the space below, write down the most significant thing you gained in this session—from the teaching, activities, or discussions.

   What I want to remember from this session . . .

Group Practice: Blessing God with Your Gratitude

We have the ability not just to bless others, but to also bless God. The grateful soul loves blessing God! The group practice this week is to train your heart to bless the Lord by expressing your gratitude to him consistently throughout the day.

- Challenge yourself to write down at least fifteen blessings each day—five in the morning, five in the afternoon, and five in the evening. For example:

  Bless you, Lord, for hot coffee in my favorite mug.

  Bless you, Lord, for how happy I feel when I hear my child laugh.

The Practice of Gratitude

Bless you, Lord, for giving me the courage to apologize.

Bless you, Lord, for being with me through this hard day.

Bless you, Lord, for giving me a beautiful sunset on my commute home tonight.

- Set aside fifteen minutes at the beginning or end of each day to reflect on your list. What effect did blessing God and writing down your gratitude have on you? Note your daily observations on a pad of paper or in a journal.

- At the end of the week, review your daily blessing lists and observations. What stands out most to you about your experience of blessing God with your gratitude?

Bring your notes from the week to the next group gathering. You'll have a chance to talk about your experiences and observations at the beginning of the Session 6 discussion.

Closing Prayer

Close your time together with prayer.

Get a Head Start on the Discussion for Session 6

As part of the group discussion for Session 6, you'll have an opportunity to talk about what you've learned and experienced together throughout the *Soul Keeping* study. Between now and your next meeting, consider taking a few moments to review the previous sessions and identify the teaching, discussions, or insights that stand out most to you. Use the worksheet on the following pages to briefly summarize the highlights of what you've learned and experienced.

SESSION 6 HEAD START WORKSHEET

Take a few moments to reflect on what you've learned and experienced throughout the *Soul Keeping* study. You may want to review notes from the video teaching, what you wrote down for "What I Want to Remember" at the end of each group session, responses in the personal studies, etc. Here are some questions you might consider as part of your review:

- What insights did I gain from this session?
- What was the most important thing I learned about myself in this session?
- How did I experience God's presence or leading related to this session?
- How did this session impact my relationships with the other people in the group?

Use the spaces provided below and on the next page to briefly summarize what you've learned and experienced for each session.

SESSION 1: What Is the Soul?

SESSION 2: The Struggle of the Soul

SESSION 3: What the Soul Needs

SESSION 4: The Practice of Grace

SESSION 5: The Practice of Gratitude

SESSION 5: Personal Study

Read and Learn

Read chapters 12–15 of the book *Soul Keeping*. Use the space below to note any insights or questions you want to bring to the next group session.

Study and Reflect

> More gratitude will not come from acquiring more things or experiences, but from more of an awareness of God's presence and his goodness. It's a way of looking at life, always perceiving the good.
>
> *Soul Keeping*, page 166

1. The promise of Scripture is that literally every good thing we have and enjoy is a gift. All of it comes directly from the God who "richly provides us with everything for our enjoyment" (1 Timothy 6:17).

Practice perceiving the good by identifying at least ten things you are grateful for in this moment. Here are some categories you might consider:

Physical health	Technology
Home	Nature
Family/friends	Education
Employment	Experiences/opportunities
Food	Talents/skills

EXAMPLES:
I am grateful for. . .
    The clean, hot water I showered in this morning.
    Having a good friend to go running with.
    The quiet and rest I feel in this moment.

I am grateful for . . .

1.

2.

3.

4.

5.

6.

7.

8.

9.

10.

---

2. Briefly review your gratitude list. How does the list as a whole impact your awareness of God's presence and God's goodness in your life?

Consider how your life might be different if you suddenly no longer had these things. How does this influence your feelings of gratitude for them or your ability to see them as God's gifts?

The default mode of the sinful human race is entitlement, the belief that this gift or that experience that God placed in my path is rightfully mine. I am owed.

Here's the deal: The more you think you're entitled to, the less you will be grateful for. The bigger the sense of entitlement, the smaller the sense of gratitude.

Soul Keeping, page 168

3. The gospel of Luke includes this compelling story about gratitude.

Now on his way to Jerusalem, Jesus traveled along the border between Samaria and Galilee. As he was going into a village, ten men who had leprosy met him. They stood at a distance and called out in a loud voice, "Jesus, Master, have pity on us!"

When he saw them, he said, "Go, show yourselves to the priests." And as they went, they were cleansed.

One of them, when he saw he was healed, came back, praising God in a loud voice. He threw himself at Jesus' feet and thanked him — and he was a Samaritan.

Jesus asked, "Were not all ten cleansed? Where are the other nine? Has no one returned to give praise to God except this foreigner?" Then he said to him, "Rise and go; your faith has made you well." (Luke 17:11 – 19)

Jesus commends the man who returns, but not before he first points out that the man is a "foreigner," specifically a Samaritan — someone Jews would have despised and considered pagan. How might this fact figure into the man's sense of entitlement as well as his expression of gratitude?

What might the entitlement implications be for the nine who did not return? How do you think it's possible to take such a gift for granted?

In what ways do you recognize yourself in the response of the one who returned? For example, what strong expression of gratitude and praise have you offered to God recently? In what ways did the experience of giving thanks and praise add to your experience of the gift itself or strengthen your relationship with God?

In what ways do you recognize yourself in the response of the nine who did not return? For example, what gifts (perhaps even some you listed in response to question 1) do you tend to take for granted or perhaps feel entitled to? What do you think you might be missing out on in your relationship with God as a result?

---

4. Read Psalm 145 in which the psalmist gives extravagant praise and thanks to God for his goodness and his mighty acts. Drawing on the psalm as a reference, use the space below to write your own prayer. Ask God to help you develop the habit of routinely recognizing the good. Be extravagant in praise and thanks for God's goodness to you. Put your heart into it! Every blessing you have is God's gift to you, and he loves to hear you say thank you.

THE PRACTICE OF GROWTH

If [God] is pleased with anything it is with the growth of the soul.

ST. JOHN OF THE CROSS, *THE SPIRITUAL CANTICLE*
OF THE SOUL AND THE BRIDEGROOM CHRIST

Group Discussion: Checking In (20 minutes)

A key part of getting to know God better is sharing your journey with others. Before watching the video, check in with each other about your experiences since the last session. For example:

- Briefly share your experience of the Session 5 group practice. What did you learn or experience from blessing God with your gratitude?

- What insights did you discover in the personal study or in the chapters you read from the book *Soul Keeping*?

- How did the last session impact your daily life or your relationship with God?

- What questions would you like to ask the other members of your group?

Video: The Practice of Growth (22 minutes)

Play the video segment for Session 6. As you watch, use the outline provided to follow along or to take additional notes on anything that stands out to you.

Notes

"When you were younger you dressed yourself and went where you wanted; but when you are old you will stretch out your hands, and someone else will dress you and lead you where you do not want to go" (John 21:18).

Because the soul is the deepest expression of the person, the soul is the seat of greatest pain.

What is the dark night of the soul?

The phrase "dark night of the soul" comes from a Carmelite monk named John of the Cross who lived in Spain in the sixteenth century.

The Dark Night of the Soul is an account of how God works to change us not just through joy and light, but in confusion, disappointment, and loss.

The dark night of the soul is not just suffering; it is suffering in what feels like the silence of God.

There will come a time when God removes the previous consolation of the soul in order to teach it virtue.

In the dark night, the soul is pained but not hopeless.

"God's love is not content to leave us in our weakness, and for this reason he takes us into the dark night. He weans us from all of the pleasures by giving us dry times and inward darkness ... no soul will ever grow deep in the spiritual life unless God works passively in that soul by means of the dark night" (St. John of the Cross).

We lack the patience that waits for whatever God would give, whenever God chooses to give.

"This will be a test of your joyful confidence in God" (Dallas Willard).

When she heard about Dallas Willard's failing health, Joni Eareckson Tada sent him these words from nineteenth-century writer Frederick Faber:

> In the spiritual life [God chooses] to try our patience first of all by his slowness.... He is slow: we are swift and precipitate. It is because we are but for a time, and he has been from eternity....
>
> There is something greatly overawing in the extreme slowness of God. Let it overshadow our souls, but let it not disquiet them.... We must wait for God, long, meekly, in the wind and wet, in the thunder and the lightning, in the cold and the dark. Wait, and he will come. He never comes to those who do not wait. He does not go to their road. When he comes, go with him, but go slowly, fall a little behind; when he quickens his pace, be sure of it, before you quicken yours. But when he slackens, slacken at once. And do not be slow only, but silent, very silent, for he is God.[16]

---

16. Frederick Faber, *Growth in Holiness* (Baltimore: John Murphy and Co., 1855), 116, 117, 120.

We practice growth by going slowly and letting silence have its way. We do nothing. We wait and we remember that we are not God. We go slowly and quietly. We wait on the goodness of God.

The apostle Paul spoke of redeeming time: "Be very careful, then, how you live — not as unwise but as wise, making the most of every opportunity, because the days are evil" (Ephesians 5:15–16).

The reason our souls hunger so is that the life we could be living so far exceeds our wildest dreams.

Dallas said he regretted all the time he wasted, not because he was comparing himself with other people or with efficiency, but because he began to see what life *could be*.

"All of us lost souls allow ourselves to live in worry and anger and self-importance and pettiness and stupidity when life with God — glory — is all around us. Your time is already in the pawnshop of lost souls" (Dallas Willard).

Characteristics of a restored soul:

- It is able to say yes or no without anxiety or duplicity.
- It is able to speak with calm confidence and honesty.
- It is willing to disappoint anybody if needed, but it's ready to bless everybody.
- It has a mind filled with more noble thoughts — just good thoughts — than could ever be spoken.
- It shares without thinking.
- It sees without being judgmental.
- It is so genuinely humble that each person seen is an object of wonder.

Dallas once said, "The gospel means that this universe is a perfectly safe place for you to be." It means that the soul is simply not at risk — not even from cancer. What else could Paul have meant when he said nothing can separate us from the love of God? Why else would Jesus have advised us not to worry?

"I think after I die, it may be some time before I realize it.... A person, a soul, is mostly a series of conscious experiences — you are not mostly your body, you're alive to reality, and this will not stop even when you die. That's why Jesus said that the one who trusts him will never taste death" (Dallas Willard).

The stream is your soul. And you are the keeper.

Group Discussion (44 minutes)

Take time to talk about what you just watched.

1. What part of the teaching had the most impact on you?

The Dark Night of the Soul

2. Despite all he had suffered and lost in the aftermath of a stroke, John's friend Dieter affirmed his life as "good"—that it was well with his soul.

Imagine for a moment that there are two Dieters—two men who have suffered precisely the same tragedy and irreversible hardships. The only difference between them is that one is able to see his life as good and the other cannot; one affirms his soul as well and the other does not.

- If circumstances are equally severe for both men, would you say they suffer equally? In what ways, if any, might the two men experience their suffering differently?

- Many Christians affirm that their greatest growth has come in times of suffering. If we assume that spiritual growth alone is what accounts for the difference between the two men, how would you describe that growth? What, specifically, do you think makes it possible for one man to say it is well with his soul?

3. What distinguishes the dark night of the soul from other kinds of suffering is the sense that God is silent. Experiences of prayer, Bible reading, and worship that once brought comfort or a sense of connection to God no longer do. According to John of the Cross, God has a clear purpose in these deprivations:

> God perceives the imperfections within us, and because of his love for us, urges us to grow up. His love is not content to leave us in our weakness, and for this reason he takes us into a dark night. He weans us from all of the pleasures by giving us dry times and inward darkness.... No soul will ever grow deep in the spiritual life unless God works passively in that soul by means of the dark night.[17]

- How do you respond to the idea that there are times God works passively, through absence rather than presence? Is this a new idea to you or something you're familiar with?

---

17. St. John of the Cross, *The Dark Night of the Soul*, excerpted in *Devotional Classics*, Richard J. Foster and James Bryan Smith, eds. (SanFrancisco: HarperSanFrancisco, 1990, 1991, 1993), 36.

- How does the metaphor of being weaned shed light on God's purpose in the dark night?

- If you have experienced a dark night of the soul, how would you describe it? What growth did you experience that you might not have experienced any other way?

4. At the start of a dark night experience, some develop what John of the Cross described as "spiritual greed." They intensify their spiritual activity in an effort to gain more spiritual consolation. He writes:

> They will become discontented with what God gives them because they do not experience the consolation they think they deserve.... Their hearts grow attached to the feelings they get from their devotional life. They focus on the affect, and not the substance of devotion.... But those who are on the right path will set their eyes on God and not on ... their inner experiences. They will enter the dark night of the soul and find all of these things removed. They will have all pleasure taken away so that the soul may be purified. For a soul will never grow until it is able to let go of the tight grasp it has on God.[18]

---

18. *The Dark Night of the Soul,* 34–35.

- How would you distinguish what John of the Cross termed "spiritual greed" from an authentic desire for God?

- Do you think it's possible to sincerely believe we are being devoted to God when what we really have is devotion to self, cloaked in spiritual activities? Share the reasons for your response.

- Within the context John of the Cross describes, what do you think it means to have a "tight grasp" on God? How might it differ from clinging to God in authentic trust?

5. When John shared his own dark night experience, Dallas responded, "This will be a test of your joyful confidence in God." To be joyful is to have a deep sense of happiness and well-being. To have confidence is to believe that someone will act in a trustworthy way.

   Why do you think Dallas included the word *joyful* in his statement? How might your understanding of his statement be different if he had merely said, "This will be a test of your confidence in God"?

What Life Could Be

6. At the end of his life, Dallas said he regretted all the time he wasted, not because he was comparing himself with other people or with efficiency, but because he began to see what life *could be*. He said:

> All of us lost souls allow ourselves to live in worry and anger and self-importance and pettiness and stupidity when life with God—glory—is all around us. Your time is already in the pawnshop of lost souls.

The appeal of a pawnshop is quick cash—but it comes at a price. In exchange for personal property, customers get a high-interest loan, typically for a fraction of the item's actual value.

• Briefly consider the circumstances and conditions of a person who might use the services of a pawnshop. What parallels do you recognize between such a person and what Dallas described as the state of the lost soul?

• Dallas says we routinely pawn our time—our life with God—for lesser things. What would you say are some of the lesser things you are allowing yourself to live in right now?

7. Dallas affirmed the truth of the apostle Paul's statement about "redeeming the time":

> Therefore watch carefully how you walk, not as unwise, but as wise; redeeming the time, because the days are evil. (Ephesians 5:15–16 WEB)

The Greek word Paul uses that is translated "redeeming" is *exagorazō* (ex-ag-or-ad'-zo). It is rooted in the noun *agora* and the verb *agorazō*, which mean "market place" and "to buy in the market place." *Exagorazō* means not just to buy but to *buy back*, to redeem. By using an intensive form of the verb, Paul encourages his readers to "'buy up intensively,' to snap up every opportunity that comes."[19] This sense of the verb is evident in the Amplified translation:

> Look carefully then how you walk! Live purposefully *and* worthily *and* accurately, not as the unwise *and* witless, but as wise (sensible, intelligent people), making the very most of the time [buying up each opportunity], because the days are evil. (Ephesians 5:15–16 AMP)

• There is urgency in Paul's statement but also hope — it *is* possible to redeem the time! In your own life, what comes to mind when you think about "making the very most" of your time? What are the "opportunities" you want to buy up?

• Those who are wise live *purposefully, worthily,* and *accurately.* As you imagine what life with God could be — and how your soul might be transformed — which of these words do you feel most drawn to?

---

19. David H. Field, *"exagorazō,"* New International Dictionary of New Testament Theology, vol. 1, Colin Brown, gen. ed. (Grand Rapids: Zondervan, 1967, 1969, 1971), 267–268.

• What connections do you recognize between the word you chose and what you most need or desire from God right now?

Souls in Community

8. Take a few moments to discuss what you've learned and experienced together throughout the *Soul Keeping* study.

   • What would you say is the most important thing you learned or experienced? How has it impacted you? For example, in your attitudes, behaviors, relationships, etc.

   • How have you recognized God at work in your life through the study?

   • At the end of every session, you had an opportunity to talk about what you needed from the other members of the group and how you could be good companions for one another. What changes, if any, have you noticed in the ways you interact with each other now compared to the beginning of the study?

Individual Activity: **What I Want to Remember** (2 minutes)

Complete this activity on your own.

1. Briefly review the video outline and any notes you took.

2. In the space below, write down the most significant thing you gained in this session—from the teaching, activities, or discussions.

   What I want to remember from this session . . .

Group Practice: **Taking Your Soul Seriously**

You are a soul made by God, made for God, and made to need God. Therefore, you must "own" your soul and take responsibility before God for it. This is the principle teaching of the *Soul Keeping* study. The group practice for this final session is to set aside a block of time— anywhere from an hour to a day—to pray and reflect on what it means in practical terms for you to take your soul seriously. Even if you aren't able to do so in the week ahead, block a specific time on your calendar when you will do so. The goal is to identify your next right step, however small, and then to take it. If you have trouble identifying a next step, here are a few options to consider.

- Choose one or more of the group practice disciplines (from sessions 1–5) that was meaningful to you and continue to practice it.

- Explore a new spiritual practice, such as simplicity, Sabbath observance, confession, spending time in solitude and silence, or meditative reading of Scripture (*lectio divina*). For additional guidance, consult *The Spiritual Disciplines Handbook* or other resources listed at the back of this study guide.

- Eliminate hurry. Simplify your life by gracefully disengaging from one or more commitments or distractions that make it difficult for you to care for your soul. In the spiritual life, saying no to externals is often the best way of saying yes to God.

- Seek out intentional relationships for confession, care, and guidance. This might be a Christian counselor, a spiritual director, a spiritual friend, or a study or support group focused on a specific life issue.

- Deepen your knowledge about the soul and spiritual transformation in Christ by reading books about the spiritual life. For options, see the list of Additional Resources at the back of this guide.

If your group is ongoing, allow time during your next gathering to talk about your experiences of taking your soul seriously and identifying your next right step. If this is your last group meeting, commit to sharing your experience with a friend or another member of the group one-on-one. Encourage and pray for one another in the days ahead.

Closing Prayer

Close your time together with prayer.

SESSION 6: Personal Study

Read and Learn

Read chapters 16–17 of the book *Soul Keeping*. Use the space below to note any insights or questions.

Study and Reflect

> The reason our souls hunger so is that the life we could be living so far exceeds our strangest dreams.
>
> *Soul Keeping*, page 186

---

1. In *Renovation of the Heart*, Dallas Willard provides a compelling picture of restored souls and of the life our souls are hungry for. He refers to such souls as "children of light" (Ephesians 5:8–11). "They are not perfect," he writes, "but they are remarkably different." These differences are evident in every dimension of life discussed throughout the *Soul Keeping* study — the will, the mind, the body, and the soul.

In the sidebar, "A Composite Picture of the Children of Light," read through Willard's descriptions one at a time. As you read, resist focusing on the ways you fall short and focus instead on what you long for — the kind of life you want to live. After reading each description, use the prompts that follow the sidebar to reflect on each of these areas in your own life.

A Composite Picture of the Children of Light*

The Will: They are devoted to doing what is good and right. Their will is habitually attuned to it, just as their mind and emotions are habitually homing in on God. They are attentive to rightness, to kindness, to helpfulness, and they are purposefully knowledgeable about life, about what people need, and about how to do what is right and good in appropriate ways. These are people who do not think first of themselves and what they want, and they care very little, if at all, about getting their own way.... They are abandoned to God's will and do not struggle and deliberate as to whether they will do what they know to be wrong. They do not hesitate to do what they know to be right. It is the obvious thing to do.

The Mind: Simply stated, they think about God. He is never out of their mind. They love to dwell upon God and upon his greatness and loveliness, as brought to light in Jesus Christ. They adore him in nature, in history, in his Son and in his saints.... They do not dwell upon evil. It is not a big thing in their thoughts.... Because their mind is centered upon God and oriented with reference to him, all other good things are also welcome there (Philippians 4:8).... They are positive, realistically so, based on the nature of God as they understand it.

Their emotional life is characterized by love. They love lots of good things and they love people.... They love their life and who they are. They are thankful for their life—even though it may contain many difficulties.... They receive all of it as God's gift.... Joy and peace are with them even in the hardest of times—even when suffering unjustly. Because of what they have learned about God, they are confident and hopeful and do not indulge thoughts of rejection, failure, and hopelessness, because *they know better.*

The Body: Their body has come over to the side of their will to do good. It is constantly *poised* to do what is right and good without thinking. And that means it does not automatically move into what is wrong, even contrary to their resolves and intentions, before they can think to *not* do it.... Consequently, we do not see them always being trapped by what their tongue, facial expressions, eyes, hands, and so on have *already* done before they can think.... The bodies of these people even *look* different. There is a freshness about them, a kind of quiet strength, and a transparency. They are rested and playful in a bodily strength that is from God.

The Soul: As you come to know these people ... you see that all of the above is not just at the surface. It is deep, and in a certain obvious sense, it is effortless. It *flows*. [These] are not things children of light are constantly trying hard to do, gritting their teeth and carrying on. Instead, these are features of life that well up out of a soul that is at home in God.... It doesn't mean perfection, but it does mean we have here a person whose soul is whole: a person who, through the internalized integrity of the law of God and the administrations of the gospel and the Spirit, has a restored soul.

*Excerpted from Dallas Willard, *Renovation of the Heart*, 218–220.

My Will

What I most want to be true in this area of my life . . .

My Mind

What I most want to be true in this area of my life . . .

My Body

What I most want to be true in this area of my life . . .

My Soul

What I most want to be true in this area of my life . . .

The eternal life that begins with confidence in Jesus is a life in his present kingdom, now on earth and available to all.... Our future, however far we look, is a natural extension of the faith by which we live now and the life in which we now participate. Eternity is now in flight and we with it, like it or not.

Dallas Willard, *The Divine Conspiracy*, page xvii

2. If your future — even into eternity — is a natural extension of your life and faith now, what kinds of things might you expect to be true of you in both the near and the distant future?

What kinds of things need to begin to be true now in order for you to grow into the kind of life you described in question 1?

3. Read Psalm 84, in which the psalmist describes how the soul longs to be with God, and the blessings that come to those "whose hearts are set on pilgrimage." Drawing on the psalm as a reference, use the space below to write a prayer that expresses your own desire for God and the kind of life you want to have with him. Acknowledge your struggles, weaknesses, and disappointments. Ask him to restore your soul and to lead you into the next right step.

Additional Resources

Books by Dallas Willard (www.dwillard.org)

Hearing God: Developing a Conversational Relationship with God (1984, 1999)

The Spirit of the Disciplines: Understanding How God Changes Lives (1988)

The Divine Conspiracy: Rediscovering Our Hidden Life in God (1998)

Renovation of the Heart: Putting on the Character of Christ (2002)

The Great Omission: Rediscovering Jesus' Essential Teachings on Discipleship (2006)

Knowing Christ Today: Why We Can Trust Spiritual Knowledge (2009)

Spiritual Formation and Spiritual Practices

Answering God: The Psalms as Tools for Prayer, Eugene H. Peterson

Celebration of Discipline: The Path to Spiritual Growth, Richard J. Foster

The Good and Beautiful God: Falling in Love with the God Jesus Knows, James Bryan Smith

Invitation to a Journey: A Roadmap for Spiritual Formation, M. Robert Mulholland, Jr.

Invitation to Solitude and Silence: Experiencing God's Transforming Presence, Ruth Haley Barton

Life Together: The Classic Exploration of Faith in Community, Dietrich Bonhoeffer

Life with God: Reading the Bible for Spiritual Transformation, Richard J. Foster

The Life You've Always Wanted: Spiritual Disciplines for Ordinary People, John Ortberg

The Me I Want to Be: Becoming God's Best Version of You, John Ortberg

One Thousand Gifts: A Dare to Live Fully Right Where You Are, Ann Voskamp

Prayer: Finding the Heart's True Home, Richard J. Foster

Sabbath: The Ancient Practices Series, Dan Allender

Sacred Companions: The Gift of Spiritual Friendship and Direction, David G. Benner

Sacred Pathways: Discover Your Soul's Path to God, Gary Thomas

Sacred Rhythms: Arranging Our Lives for Spiritual Transformation, Ruth Haley Barton

Sanctuary of the Soul: Journey into Meditative Prayer, Richard J. Foster

Soul Feast: An Invitation to the Christian Spiritual Life, Marjorie Thompson

Soul Keeping: Caring for the Most Important Part of You, John Ortberg

Spiritual Direction and the Care of Souls, Gary W. Moon and David G. Benner

Spiritual Direction: Wisdom for the Long Walk of Faith, Henri J. M. Nouwen

Spiritual Disciplines Handbook: Practices That Transform Us, Adele Ahlberg Calhoun

Spiritual Formation: Following the Movements of the Spirit, Henri J. M. Nouwen

The Way of the Heart: Connecting with God through Prayer, Wisdom, and Silence, Henri J. M. Nouwen

Spiritual Classics

The Confessions of Saint Augustine, St. Augustine

Dark Night of the Soul, Saint John of the Cross

Devotional Classics, Revised and Expanded: Selected Readings for Individuals and Groups, edited by Richard J. Foster and James Bryan Smith

The Great Divorce, C. S. Lewis

The Imitation of Christ, Thomas à Kempis

Interior Castle, St. Teresa of Avila

The Practice of the Presence of God, Brother Lawrence

The Screwtape Letters, C. S. Lewis

Spiritual Classics: Selected Readings on the Twelve Spiritual Disciplines, edited by Richard J. Foster and Emilie Griffin

A Testament of Devotion, Thomas R. Kelly

Soul Keeping

Caring for the Most Important Part of You

Bestselling Author John Ortberg

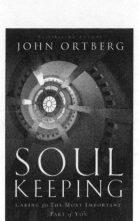

The soul is NOT "a theological and abstract subject."

The soul is the coolest, eeriest, most mysterious, evocative, crucial, sacred, eternal, life-directing, fragile, indestructible, controversial, expensive dimension of your existence.

Jesus said it's worth more than the world.

You'd be an idiot not to prize it above all else.

Shouldn't you get pretty clear on exactly what it is? Shouldn't you know what it runs on? Wouldn't it be worth knowing how to care for it?

Two things are for sure. One is: you have a soul. The other is: if you don't look after this one, you won't be issued a replacement.

Bestselling author John Ortberg writes another classic that will help readers discover their soul and take their relationship with God to the next level.

Deut 6:5 You shall love the Lord
your God with all your heart and
with all your soul and with all your
might
Matt 22: 38 - 40

p48 " take up our cross" =
   to choose self-denial, for His sake
   a lifestyle of sacrificial choices
   choices include the way I use my
   will, my mind, my body..."

p.83 what experiences did you have
   that made you feel significant,
   even in a small way?
   "How do you count in ways that
   no one else does..."

   Is 26:3

p93 " Do not despise these small
   beginnings, for the LORD rejoices
   to see the work begin..." Zech 4:10